The Principles & Processes of Interactive Design

Jamie Steane

BLOOMSBURY

Fairchild Books
An imprint of Bloomsbury Publishing Plc

50 Bedford Square
London
WC1B 3DP
UK

1385 Broadway
New York
NY 10018
USA

www.bloomsbury.com

Bloomsbury is a registered trade mark of Bloomsbury Publishing Plc

First published 2014

British Library Cataloguing-in-Publication Data
A catalogue record for this book is available from the British Library.

ISBN
PB: 978-2-940-496-11-2
ePDF: 978-2-940447-66-4

Library of Congress Cataloging-in-Publication Data
Steane, Jamie.
Principles and processes of interactive design / Jamie Steane.
pages cm
Includes bibliographical references and index.
ISBN 978-2-940496-11-2 (pbk.) -- ISBN 978-2-940447-66-4 (ePDF) 1. Commercial art--
Data processing. 2. Graphic arts--Data processing. 3. Digital media--Design. I. Title.
NK1520.S74 2014
741.6--dc23
2013020876

Designed by Struktur Design Limited
Printed and bound in China

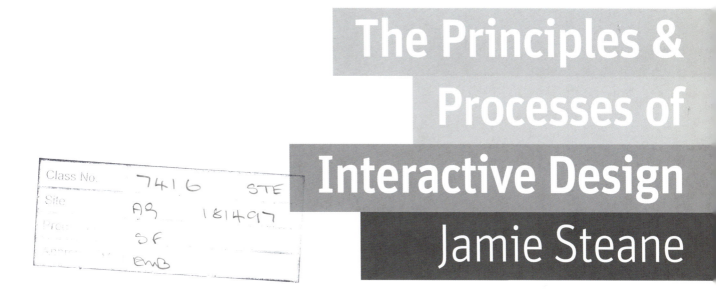

The Principles & Processes of Interactive Design

Jamie Steane

BLOOMSBURY

Introduction

For many of us living in the information age, the digital revolution has had a significant impact on how we live, work and play. In the world of design, its impact has transformed design practices and created new opportunities; it has revolutionized traditional analogue processes, such as printing and model-making; and has created new design disciplines, including web design and computer animation. It has also provided new challenges and problems for design to solve: for example, how do we design a smartphone interface or harness the power of social media to promote a brand?

The Principles & Processes of Interactive Design is aimed at new designers from across the design and media disciplines, who want to learn the fundamentals of designing for interactive media. This book is intended both as a primer and companion guide on how to research, plan and design for increasingly prevalent interactive projects.

0.01–0.04 | Ollo interactive logo
To help create an emotional connection between new telecommunications brand Ollo and its audience, Bibliothèque have designed an interactive logo that reflects its engaging and playful brand values.

What *is* interactive design?

According to the UK's Design Council, 48% of design agencies in the UK undertake 'digital and multimedia' work, despite the incredible fact that the discipline barely existed less than 20 years earlier (Design Industry 2010 study). Perceptions of what interactive design actually is have also changed with each new major technological development.

The digital revolution

Whether you are a graphic designer developing a website, a product designer creating a new app, or a budding director producing a new interactive video, it is apparent just how much the digital revolution has touched all facets of our design and production processes. Furthermore, the emergence of digital technology has also contributed to a blurring of the boundaries between design disciplines, as shared software tools and the digitization of traditional media and products have led to new forms of creative practice.

The range of different uses of digital media and the diversity of practice that exists makes it challenging to define a specific set of relevant skills and the parameters of practice that might be encapsulated within the term 'interactive design'. For the purposes of this book, Interactive Design is defined as the shaping of digital products and services for people to use, although it is recognized that the scope of interactive design extends beyond this definition to include complex systems and immersive environments too. While this book will touch upon all these opportunities for interactive design, it will take the principles and processes behind screen-based design for everyday products and services as its focus.

As digital video is predicted to account for almost 90% of all Internet traffic by 2016 according to computer networking giant Cisco Systems, the importance of understanding how to design for video and television will also be emphasized throughout this book as part of an integrated media approach to *The Principles & Processes of Interactive Design*.

0.05 | Spotify: An online music streaming service
The digital age replaced the ownership of many physical products and notions of ownership with virtual interfaces and subscription-based services.

0.06 | Little Printer
An adorable hack of new
and old technologies by
Berg: this is a thermal
printer reminiscent of the
1980s, with twenty-first
century Wi-Fi connectivity.

What this book does

The blurring of boundaries between design disciplines is leading to a new breed of hybrid designers, who retain strong interests in their core discipline while also developing a greater understanding of general design principles and processes in this convergent digital space. It is these common principles and processes that we shall explore over the course of this book, which explores the design fundamentals of design research and development, in addition to individual visual design elements such as colour, image, typography and layout. As with interactive design itself, this book's structure comprises a hybrid of logical processes and creative endeavour.

Chapter 1, *Research for Interaction*, re-interprets established design processes through a digital lens, with the aim of helping you to understand the importance of the individual 'user' – rather than the more generalized views of audiences – when designing interaction. This chapter includes an industry perspective that is designed to give you further insights into how these processes and principles have been applied in a real-world scenario; a workshop activity follows so that you can learn how to apply them in your own practice.

The second chapter focuses on *Design Development* and explores the early and middle design development phases that exist prior to producing more finished visual designs. It describes information sorting and site-mapping methods, as well as different forms of prototyping and storyboarding **ideas**. This chapter also emphasizes the importance of user testing and demonstrates how crucial it is in informing the design process.

In *Colour and Image*, you are taken through the basics of colour, image meaning and manipulation, as well as the technical differences between designing for print and digital. This third chapter also explains how to use colour and encode images with meaning.

Chapter 4 focuses on *Digital Typography* and discusses the most important considerations when selecting type and manipulating text on screen. For example, serif fonts are infrequently used on television due to legibility issues, while **copy** is written in bite sizes on the web to allow for scan reading and search engine optimization.

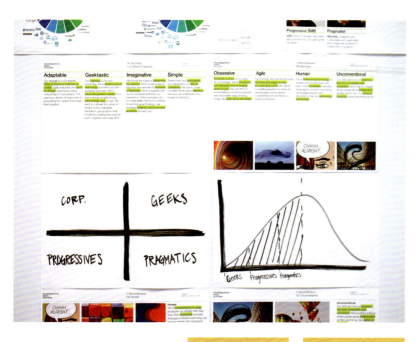

0.07 | Research for interaction
Brand behaviours and brand characters are considered alongside the customer profiles by Moving Brands.

0.08 | Colour and image
Images generated using a bespoke software application created by design agency Onformative in co-operation with Interbrand.

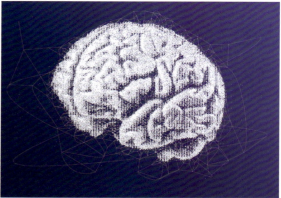

Next, Chapter 5 explores *Grids and Layouts* and draws together the principles of composition. It provides a historical overview of the development of grid systems and considers this in relation to the latest thinking on responsive layouts for desktop and mobile platforms. In addition, it also details the screen sizes and guidelines associated with different forms of interactive design layout.

Chapter 6, *Interactive Formats*, showcases different uses of on-screen interactive design and touches upon formats without boundaries, as interaction moves beyond the small screen into environments and events. These examples are integrated with relevant interaction theory on the design of learnable interfaces, mobile application development and games design so that readers can learn to create designs that are relevant to user needs and the contexts within which they will be used.

The final chapter looks at *Presenting Your Ideas*, with a view to giving aspiring digital designers an insight into how professional designers present their design work to clients and in their portfolios. The chapter covers practical topics on presentation formats and communicating your ideas, as well as providing visual examples of presentations and folios.

As you read through this book, you will find many commonly used specialist terms highlighted in bold; these are defined in the glossary towards the end of this book, where there is also a comprehensive bibliography and useful resources section to further enhance your learning.

It is hoped that this book will provide valuable insights into how essential principles and processes inform interactive design for those who are new to the subject, as well as for the more experienced designer; and that the plethora of visual examples and industry perspectives will provide stimulation for your ongoing creative work.

0.09 | Digital typography
e-Types create a typographic identity, with a new typeface and web font, for Jazzhouse in Copenhagen.

0.10 | Grids and layouts
This is Kinetic's playful homepage, which uses parallax scrolling to create a visually dynamic experience.

Research for interaction

Designers are often keen to shy away from digital media projects, perhaps because they have a tendency to falsely equate technology with a lack of creativity. Yet, technology and creativity should not be seen as diametrically opposed to one another; each new technical innovation actually brings with it a wealth of new creative opportunities to explore.

The relentless pace of technological change does, however, mean that digital media projects are often complex, because how audiences or end users will respond to new developments cannot be easily anticipated without solid research and development.

This is particularly the case for interactive projects, such as building a website or designing an app, where **user experience (UX)** is more likely to be active rather than passive. Unlike reading a magazine or watching a DVD, where a certain type of consumer use and responsive behaviour may be assumed, navigating a new website can be similar to handling an unfamiliar appliance for users. Building a new website therefore requires careful research and user testing as part of an iterative design process in order to ensure that users can access its content and use its functions in the most effective and rewarding way.

In this chapter, we will explore a range of research techniques and strategies that may prove vital when performing design research for an interactive project. First, we will look at the need to interrogate the brief as a starting point for effective research before going on to explore the importance of market research, audience research and visual research.

1.1–1.6 | Brand and user experience workshop

These photos taken during a brand workshop with Plump Digital's client, Ardent Financial Planning, show a range of research techniques that help both designers and clients to evaluate current brand position and user experiences prior to starting new design work.

Top row: A 'warm-up' exercise identifying car brand values helps to sharpen clients' analytical skills before they then learn to apply them to their own brand.

Middle row: Competitors' visual identities, marketing material and websites are analysed to help evaluate their relative strengths and weaknesses.

Bottom row: A brand matrix is a visual way to compare brands using selected criteria. The drawing of customer journey maps helps designers and clients understand how users interact with brand and service touchpoints over time.

Research methods available to the designer

Market research	User research	Visual research
Brand matrix	A day in the life	**Blogs**
Competitor analysis	Co-design	Brand colour maps
Context review	Contextual interviews	Colour prediction
Cool hunting	Customer journeys	**Culture hunt**
Questionnaires and surveys	**Cultural probes**	**Desktop moodboards**
Segmentation research	Expectation maps	Desktop walk-through
Viral market research	**Focus groups**	Empathy tools
Web analytics	**Personas**	Filming
	Scenarios	Graphic facilitation
	Interviews	Moodboards
	Mobile ethnography	Service safari
	Photo ethnography	**Shared inspiration**
	Relationship mapping	**Sketchbooks**
	Shadowing	Storyboards
	User stories	
	Visual anthropology	

The table shows a number of research methods available to the designer: those highlighted in bold are explained in this chapter.

Understanding the brief

Although it may seem obvious, understanding the brief is absolutely vital to the success of a project. Misinterpretation caused by not asking the right questions at the briefing stage, or from not researching the brief thoroughly enough, are common mistakes made by inexperienced designers.

A good brief will articulate the project aims, requirements, intended audience, timescales, budget and, increasingly, the criteria by which success will be measured. A great brief will also supply relevant background information and explain where this project fits into a wider design strategy. To avoid costly misunderstandings, some design agencies therefore prefer to supply their clients with a tried-and-tested brief **pro forma** to make sure that they capture all the essential information in a consistent format that their design team can then quickly and easily interpret.

When reading a brief, or receiving a briefing presentation, we often look for guidance on three key areas of research: project context, focus and process. Project context is background research on the client's business; this might include its history, competitors, and current and future trends within its industry.

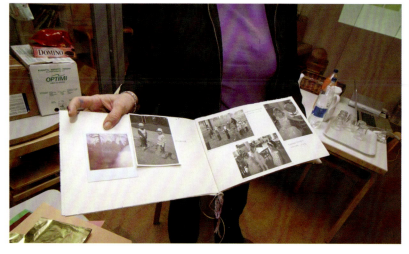

1.7–1.9 | Better every day at day care with NFC

The Finnish agency Nordkapp worked closely with their clients to help shape the brief as part of the EU-funded Smart Urban Spaces research initiative. The Nappula project aims to test and research how to best utilize contactless technologies (such as radio frequency identification (RFID) and near field identification (NFC)) in day-care centres. The goal of the project is to find better practices for the daily administrative routines, such as monitoring presence, and thus free time for the children.

Top left: Workshops with the day-care staff and parents.
Top right (2): Service definition and touch points identified.

The project focus is the specific aim of the project and any particular requirements of it – for example: 'The aim of the project is to promote our new organic grocery store and we require a web presence and digital campaign to achieve this.' The project process refers to the research methods and strategy that you will use in order to achieve the project's aims.

The project's aims and objectives are a fertile area of exploration for designers, as clients can often specify an unsuitable design solution as the answer to their problem – for example: 'We need an app to promote our new organic grocery store.' An app may or may not be the right solution to the company's marketing problems; working with the client to write an appropriate brief that will help to achieve the intended result is therefore both a necessary and important part of a designer's work.

At this stage, do not be afraid to ask simple questions:
– What is the purpose of your business?
– Who is your intended audience?
– Why do you think you need a digital campaign?
– How would your audience benefit from using your app?

Ask these questions of as many decision makers in your client's organization as you can, as there is no guarantee that they will have collectively shared their thoughts and agreed on a set of aims for your project. Reaching consensus on a set of shared aims and objectives is critical to the success of any proposed solution.

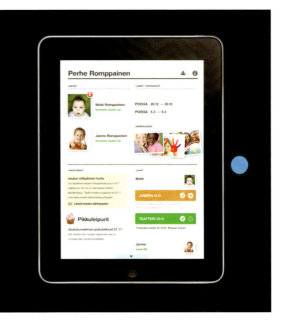

1.10–1.13 | RFID tags and user interfaces
Top images: Waterproof stickers that contain tiny Radio-Frequency Identification chips (RFID) are used to tag and identify multiple objects from individuals' keys and phones to items of children's clothing.

Bottom images: User-interfaces are created for various platforms with a separate interface created for day-care staff.

Market research

Market research refers to the systematic planning, gathering and analysis of information about a particular product or service. Market research utilizes a collection of research methods to shed light both on consumer behaviour and on market competition. Market research is a key strategic tool used in business decision-making and is an important component of design research. Market research can be undertaken by a client's own marketing department, commissioned separately, or may form part of a design brief. Where market research is unavailable, a designer is often expected to undertake basic market research to provide 'project context' and inform their design decision-making. The following selection of market research methods may prove helpful to you when making your initial design decisions.

Context review

A context or literature review is a comprehensive study of corporate literature, articles, papers, reports and books on your client, their industry and their competitors. The point of a review is to familiarize yourself with your client's history and market position. It also provides a safeguard against presenting ideas that have been tried before. For design students who are unfamiliar with performing this kind of review, a visit to see the college or university librarian is a good place to start. They will help you to become familiar with the tools and resources that are available to help you carry out a context review.

1.14 | Context review
To design successful interactive projects, you will need to understand your client's business and the customers for their services and products. Immerse yourself in relevant books and literature or elicit knowledge from your clients and their customers where possible.

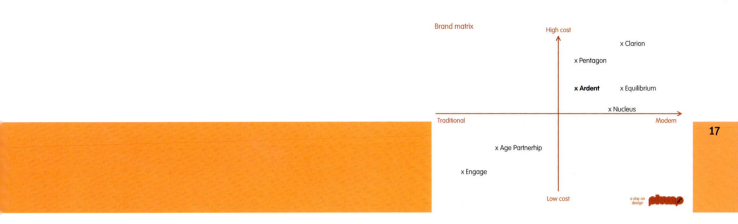

Questionnaires and surveys

Where time (and budget) allows, a questionnaire or survey may be used to gain new quantitative market intelligence. The difference between a questionnaire and a survey simply comes down to who fills out the form: a participant fills out a questionnaire, whereas a researcher questioning a participant fills out a survey.

Questionnaires or surveys work well when participants are asked about current or previous use of a product or service. Try to avoid asking leading questions, or asking participants to speculate about their future use of a new service, because what they say they 'might' do and what they actually would do often prove to be two very different things! If you do want to ask speculative questions, setting up a focus group might be a more appropriate research method to use, as this will allow you to explore the respondents' answers and motivations more thoroughly.

Brand matrix

A brand matrix is an important visualization method that informs market research. Brand matrices essentially allow designers and their clients to visualize a brand's values relative to its competition.

Two important criteria are chosen for the axes of a matrix and are labelled with appropriate scales. The brand and its competition are then plotted against these criteria in order to visualize their relative value. Distinctiveness is the ideal marketing quality for a brand: those brands that are closely clustered in the same area of the matrix will be less distinct and will invariably face the most competition.

Use brand matrices to plot important criteria for your own digital project. For example, you could use them to compare the form versus the function of websites, or the cost versus the features of video games.

1.15 | Visualizing a brand matrix
This brand matrix by Plump Digital was produced during a client workshop. By asking a client to assess their relative position to their competitors, using key criteria for their customers, their brand value and position can be visualized. They can be highly subjective without real data, but they are extremely useful for discussing brand positioning.

1.16 | Online questionnaires
Sites such as SurveyMonkey provide simple and quick ways to undertake primary research.

2.3 Competitive Analysis Summary

1.17 | Competitors' products
Similar to brand matrices, scoring competitors' interactive products and services against specific criteria is a useful way to understand their relative merits.

Competitor analysis

When designing an identity for a TV channel, creating a new app game or redeveloping a website, knowing your competition is very important. If you have already performed a context review, you will have discovered who your client's competitors are, so now it is time for a little more in-depth analysis.

Select four to six competing products or services and choose some selection criteria by which to judge them. For example, if you were planning on designing a new iPhone app, you might choose look and feel, ease of use, content and functions, and value for money. Score the products in a table, take screengrabs of their key features and write down their individual strengths and weaknesses. This evaluation provides useful analysis that you can keep for reference or use in a research presentation. More importantly, you can now cherry-pick the best features to include in your design and use the selection criteria to evaluate your own design.

Web analytics

Web analytics is statistical information about user visits to websites. For designers working online, they provide an incredibly useful source of information in helping us to understand web traffic patterns and the overall effectiveness of a website.

Web analytics can tell us a range of information about site visitors, including: the number of unique and returning visitors; the average number of pages viewed; the average length of time spent on a site; the user's location; the flow of pages viewed (also known as 'clickstreams'); and the percentage of visitors who viewed the site from a mobile device. This statistical information or 'web metrics' is important in helping to judge the effectiveness of any changes to the website or increase in traffic resulting from promotional campaigns.

This level of information commonly relies on 'page tagging', whereby a small piece of code (usually a JavaScript) is inserted into every website page. Most web-hosting companies provide some form of web analytics tool when you acquire space, but the most popular free tool is Google Analytics.

1.18 | Google Analytics
One of the most popular web analytics tools used for understanding a website's visitor traffic patterns and a site's overall effectiveness.

A client who already has a website should be able to give you access to their current analytical data. Web analytics should be used on a continual basis to assess whether website changes and digital promotions are achieving measurable results.

Popular analytics tools

alexa.com/toolbar

clicky.com

crazyegg.com

google.com/analytics

haveamint.com

springmetrics.com

statcounter.com

toolbar.google.com

woopra.com

www-01.ibm.com/software/marketing-solutions/coremetrics/

1.19 | Ranking competitors' web pages
You can compare website importance and the popularity of a website using various tools on the Web, such as Google PageRank and Alexa Toolbar. Alexa Toolbar allows you to see how a web page ranks and see potential competitors through related links.

Investigating website popularity

Download Google Toolbar and Alexa Toolbar for your web browser so that you can view the popularity of websites that you visit at a glance. Google's PageRank scores pages from 0–9 based on the number and importance of incoming links from other web pages. Alexa Toolbar ranks and displays graphs of visits, and (perhaps more interestingly) also displays related links to websites with similar content, which is great for finding out more about the competition.

User research

Unlike market research methods, which give general overviews of consumer behaviour and market competition, user research methods give detailed insights into user needs and behaviours from both real and imagined end users.

Focus groups

In contrast to questionnaires, focus groups allow a researcher to gather qualitative information about a product, service or idea. A limited number of participants, usually between six and twelve, are selected from a target audience or consumer group, and their preferences, attitudes and opinions are then gathered through moderated discussions. The key benefit of a focus group over individual interviews is this element of group discussion, which can lead both to a better understanding of the focus group's perceptions and attitudes, and usefully enables problems to be identified and investigated in more detail. Care needs to be taken so that leading questions are avoided and the views of strong characters within the focus group do not unduly influence other participants.

Personas

Personas are fictional characters that represent different kinds of users within a product's or service's target audience. They are widely used in web and product design to help clients and designers visualize their audience when making decisions about design features, user experience and content.

To create personas of your own, write down a list of character names, along with some personal details, skills, aspirations and goals to accompany them. Portraits can also be drawn or chosen from **photo libraries** to help visualize them. The number of personas created should be representative of the target audience, although one typical user may become the primary focus for your design.

1.20 | CX brand development workshops
These images illustrate Moving Brands' design research and development processes for client Cloud Experience, who provide a cloud storage service.

1.21–1.22 | Definition of the brand
Stakeholder workshops are designed to discuss, question and ultimately define the brand's behaviours and characteristics.

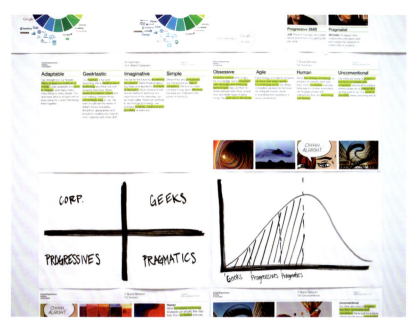

Scenarios

Scenarios are hypothetical stories about the use of a product or service, which are created in the initial research stage to inform your design. A scenario is usually a specific task given to one or all of your personas, which details every step of their experience, providing valuable insights into the requirements of your design. As a shortcut, personas and scenarios are often integrated by creating a series of personas, each with a given scenario.

Not all scenarios will have positive outcomes for your personas, as what one character might find easy and satisfying is likely to prove difficult and off-putting for another. For example, a website with a clean minimal interface employing a subtle use of typography may appeal to one technically savvy user, but to an IT novice with visual impairments it may appear obscure and difficult to read. Both positive and negative experiences tell us a lot about the content and functions that we will need to include, as well as what should be avoided.

Scenarios and competitor analysis are often used together to give insight into user experience as they generate lists of important content and functions that can then be collated to form the basis of a design. A similar alternative tool is 'user stories' – a quick method that simply states the 'who, what and why' of a potential requirement in one or two sentences.

Cultural probes

Cultural probes are information-gathering kits that allow participants to self-document a design issue that is being explored. The aim of the probe is to collect a plentiful supply of qualitative information that will inform and inspire your design. Cultural probes last a set period of time, during which participants may receive further guidance via text or email. The cultural probe can be as simple as a paper diary and pen or as sophisticated as a **smartphone**, which enables participants to take photos, record videos and write diary entries as part of a blog.

Visual research

There are many visual research methods that designers can use as sources of inspiration for a design project. The methods described below represent a small selection of those available that might be used to encourage the investigation, recording and use of visual research for digital media design projects.

Culture hunt

In contrast to cultural probes, designers gather research first-hand by visiting selected locations for a set period of time on designated culture hunts. The aim of a culture hunt is for designers to immerse themselves in places of study in order to gain insights into the design problem and so gain inspiration for a likely solution. Information can be gathered by using the same techniques as for cultural probes – that is, diaries, notebooks, cameras and sound recording equipment, as well as by undertaking impromptu interviews.

Culture hunts are often used in the physical world as a means of gaining direct experience of services and situations that need a new or improved design solution. However, it is possible to immerse yourself in a purely digital cultural hunt too. Imagine, for example, shopping for a new online bank account, trawling through discussion forums and comparison sites for advice, before assessing the online application processes for a range of different banks.

1.25–1.27 | Oral anticoagulant therapy
OATBook app by Rob Cleaton helps patients prescribed with Warfarin to monitor, track and record their medication and INR (international normalized ratio) as part of their daily routine. The images shown here are typical of photos taken during a culture hunt.

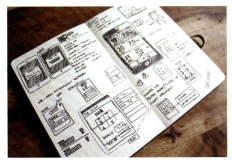

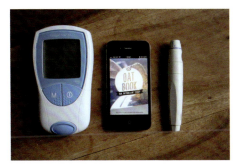

1.28–1.34 | Sketchbooks
These images illustrate elements of Rob's development process including moodboards, sketchbooks and annotated wireframe printouts.

Sketchbooks and blogs

There is still nothing to surpass a traditional sketchbook for ease and simplicity in recording notes, reference materials, thoughts and initial ideas. Keeping a sketchbook to hand for both reference purposes and for the continual development of ideas is still a vital research and development tool.

For those who may believe that the digital age has superseded the need for this analogue tool: think again! Drawing is a creative and intuitive right-side-of-the-brain activity, whereas writing is an analytical left-side activity. By using both sides, you are using the full capacity of your brain for problem solving. Drawing, therefore, actually doubles creative potential!

With this said, the digital age does allow you to harness the power of more brains by sharing your research and development with others. Digitize key pages of your sketchbook and upload them to your personal blog site. Design students are often encouraged to keep personal blogs using Tumblr or Word Press as a means of self-reflection, as well as a way of receiving helpful comments from others. Blogs are a great way of collating and sharing research and development on team-based projects, too.

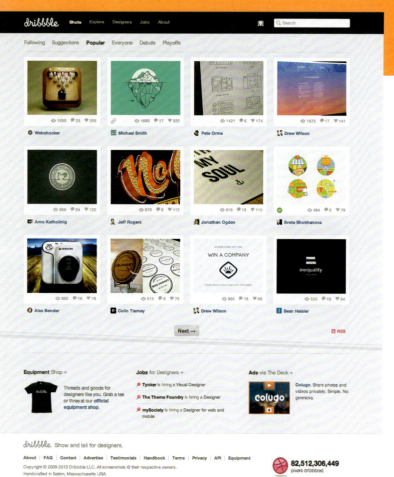

Shared inspiration

Inspiration is everywhere in this 24/7, always-online world. There is so much to see and learn at the mere press of a search button that the possibility of missing an example of creative greatness can sometimes feel overwhelming. Fortunately, it is much easier than ever before to keep track of and share sources of inspiration, thanks to an array of simple bookmarking and portfolio sites. Choosing the right resources and tools for this is a matter of personal choice – but the table here provides a selection of bookmarking and portfolio sites for you to get started with!

1.35 | Sharing and reviewing designers' work
Dribbble is a good source of inspiration for viewing the important details of designers' work, as well as providing a forum for sharing your own.

Bookmarking and portfolio sites

Bookmarking tools	Design inspiration	Design portfolios
delicious.com	artofthetitle.com	behance.net
digg.com	awwwards.com	carbonmade.com
facebook.com	designarchives.aiga.org	cargocollective.com
pinterest.com	dribbble.com	contact-creative.com
reddit.com	motionographer.com	deviantart.com
stumbleupon.com	smashingmagazine.com	sohosoho.tv
twitter.com	thefwa.com	topinteractiveagencies.com

Moodboard desktops

Traditional moodboards collaged with images cut from magazines, printed photos and colour swatches from the local hardware store have become somewhat anachronistic in the modern open-plan design studio. Moodboards are still very useful, but their form is changing as it is now much easier to simply curate them online using sites such as Pintrest, or to create moodboards using desktop software packages, which can be easily changed and stored, shared and even polished for client presentations.

Start to collect and digitize inspirational images and to reference material that you come across in books, magazines, online and so on. Organize your images into themed folders on your computer, such as by colour, image, typography and layout, or by more specialist categories such as audiences, brand language, navigation elements, art direction and so on.

Create a document the size of your desktop in Adobe Photoshop or Illustrator and place and arrange your digitized images on the canvas in order to create your moodboard. Save out a jpeg version of your finished moodboard and set it as your desktop picture.

Always be aware of copyright laws. Most professional photo libraries will allow you to use **comping images** of their photographers' and image-makers' work for the purposes of producing mock-up designs so long as images are not published or used in any commercial form. Be careful: even republishing a copyrighted image in a personal blog may be seen as an infringement. Your college librarian or tutor should be able to advise you. Alternatively, you should be able to find information about copyright laws from a number of sources online.

1.36 | Moodboard desktop
If you're a neat designer who keeps their desktop clean and tidy, a desktop moodboard might work for you.

Industry perspective:
Eilidh Dickson & Helle Rohde Andersen, CIID Consulting

Client
Novo Nordisk

Brief
To investigate the lives of Type 2 diabetes patients in the USA, with a view to discovering unaddressed user needs and new opportunities for innovation.

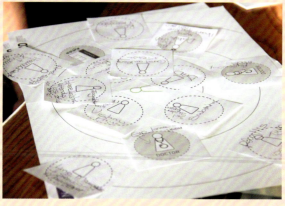

Agency
CIID Consulting (Copenhagen Institute of Interaction Design), Copenhagen, Denmark

Solution
Designers and researchers from CIID undertook in-depth field research through an approach they termed 'Immersive Living', which discovered a number of key findings that were presented through the design of an interactive iPad app.

1.37 | Using the local area
Research tool to map how the respondents use their local area.

1.38 | Network of care
Research tool to allow the respondents to map their network of care.

1.39 | Health aspirations
Card sorting exercise used to elicit future health aspirations of the respondents.

1.40 | Research documentation and analysis process

1.41 | Eilidh Dickson   **1.42 | Helle Rohde Andersen**

Interview with Eilidh Dickson and Helle Rohde Andersen
Eilidh is a Project Lead and Interaction Designer and Helle
is an Interaction and Service Designer.

Can you tell me how this project came about?
ED: Yes, Novo Nordisk wanted to gain a more in-depth
understanding of the lives of Type 2 Diabetes patients,
particularly in the USA where the condition is an increasingly
widespread problem. It was not a problem-solving exercise,
but more an exploratory brief.

**What were the main challenges for you in tackling
this brief?**
HRA: From a helicopter perspective, there were two main
challenges. The first was to take a fresh look at Type 2
Diabetes in the context of the American market. Previously,
we had worked in the field of diabetes where our research
had focused on a particular product or a very clearly
defined topic, so this was an opportunity to look at diabetes
in a more holistic way. This was the second challenge: how
do you change our approach to look at diabetes from both
a system perspective and also an individual's perspective?

How do you define a systematic approach?
ED: Normally, when we undertake research like this, we
interview a sample of people, maybe between ten and
20 people. In the case of diabetes, we would interview
patients, doctors and nurses, etc. Each interview would
happen in isolation and last up to two hours, after which
we would build a story around them.

This time we chose to use an extremely small sample of
three patients; however, we spent a week with each of them
and met with anyone who was involved in their network of care.

HRA: We called this approach 'Immersive Living'. This was
new for us because we normally go out and seek inspiration
from a multitude of stakeholders. But this was about
understanding a specific person and their network, and
then breaking down the system.

What inspired this approach?
ED: A desire to try something new. We had done a number
of projects with diabetes patients before; however, we felt
that if we went in with the same approach as before we
might end up with the same findings – we really wanted to
challenge our approach.

HRA: It was also a unique opportunity for us to design the
research approach from the beginning and treat that as the
design problem, so we came up with a set of tools to help
us with this 'Immersive Living' approach.

Industry perspective:
Eilidh Dickson & Helle Rohde Andersen, CIID Consulting

1.43 | Home page
Application home page and main navigation system.

1.44 | Scope of respondents
Dynamic visualization showing the scope of research respondents.

1.45 | Diabetes journey
Dynamic visualization showing the diabetes journey of one of the respondents.

1.46 | Diabetes treatment
Dynamic visualization communicating the facets of diabetes treatment.

1.47 | User stories
Research insights and supporting user stories.

1.48 | US health system
Dynamic visualization showing the scope of care within the US health system.

What were these tools that you used?

HRA: We wanted to design tools that would support us on an emotional level when we carried out conversations and ran activities with people.

First, we sent the patients sticky notes prior to our visit so that they could tag objects in their homes that they associated with their diabetes or that made their everyday life easier. This was a way for them to feel confident in their own home and highlight the things that they wanted to show us.

ED: Other tools included a network mapping exercise. We drew them in the middle of an A3 sheet with circles around them. Next, participants placed people or stakeholders who influenced their diabetes care on an axis, some near to them, others further away. It could be anyone from a best friend to a celebrity who inspired them to eat healthier. It enabled them to see who had helped to define their diabetes care; who they viewed as influential in this process.

We also made a 'diabetes journey' tool where the patient would map their positive and negative emotions related to their condition on a scale. We didn't use this until later in the week once we had gained participants' trust.

How did you identify your participants?

ED: The design research was undertaken in Pittsburgh, so we asked a local agency that we knew to help us recruit our participants. We didn't go through a professional recruitment company because we didn't want professional respondents.

HRA: It was a big ask and commitment for participants. We didn't just need their time, but also needed time from their friends, family and doctor so it was a large task to find people who could and would willingly give that.

How did you record your research?

ED: Apart from the work that was created from the tools, we would audio and video record everything and take photographs. Generally, we didn't take notes. At the end of each session, we would debrief and capture our thoughts. Because part of the project was visualization, we went through the mammoth task of transcribing the audio and videos.

How long did the project take from start to finish?

ED: It took five months.

What size team did you use?

ED: It varied. In the planning phase, we had the equivalent of two and a half people working full time. On the research, we had four people full time and then during the visualization we had six people, and that was a combination of researchers, designers and computer scientists.

Had you decided on designing an iPad app from the start?

ED: Actually, no. It came after we had completed the field research. We originally said that we would visualize the findings in a dynamic way, but did not specify it would be an app.

With these projects, we obviously create a presentation and an executive summary, and we usually create a coffee-table book to communicate the visual media and stories from the research. This time, because we are interaction designers, we wanted to create something interactive. After the research, it just made sense to create an interactive application since we had so much rich media in the form of videos and photos.

Workshop I:
Connected life

The following workshop is intended to help you apply some of the research methods that you have been reading about in this chapter. Working through the steps in the workshop can take you as long as you like; the minimum time it should take is in the region of three to four hours, but spending a whole day on them would be better. If you do not have that amount of time to spare, read through the brief, watch the inspirational videos and then take 20 minutes to imagine how you would complete each step.

Background

Today, we live in an increasingly complex and connected world. Technology has been a major driver behind this rapid process of change – but could it possibly simplify things too?

Now that we can watch television on our phones, download movies to our laptops and listen to podcasts on TVs, organizing our social media and personal communication is becoming an ever-more complex and time-consuming job. On the flipside, as we become more media savvy, advertisers are working harder than ever before to create meaningful dialogues with consumers in order to sell their products and services.

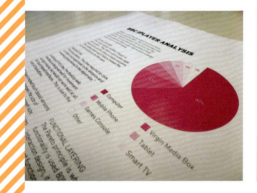

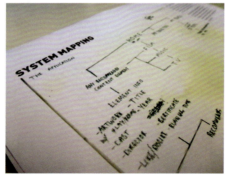

1.49–1.56 | Connected life concept
These images illustrate a response to this workshop by students David Ingledow, Max Holford and Ella Rasmussen. The team took the exercise further by developing system maps, wireframes and prototypes – topics that are covered in the next chapter on design development.

Brief

Your workshop challenge is to undertake design research for a new interactive product or service that will make life simpler for two important target audiences – 'organized parents' and the 'young tech elite'. These two audiences both have the disposable income to be able to afford to pay for a product or service that would effectively organize, make more efficient and thereby enhance their work/life balances.

Your design research will use the competition analysis, personas and scenarios outlined earlier in this chapter to provide a list of user-experience requirements for this potential new service.

Step 1 – Inspiration

Watch the following videos on YouTube to see two possible visions of the future. Search for the following terms on YouTube's homepage: Ericsson's 'The Social Web of Things'; and Microsoft's 'Future Vision' videos and 'Our LifeStyle'.

Step 2 – Competition analysis

Find six products or services that you feel can help to make technology simpler. These could include a range of services, from email clients and social media organizers, through to interactive television and online entertainment media, such as iTunes, Netflix or Spotify.

Choose a selection of criteria to judge these by: for example, look and feel, ease of use, content and functions, and value for money.

Score the products in a table, take screengrabs of key functions and write down their individual strengths and weaknesses. Make a list of potential content and functions for your service.

Step 3 – Personas

Think about the two target audiences. Using your imagination, write three short personas for each of these audiences. Give each character a name, decide how old they are, whether they are in a relationship or have a family, what they do for a living and how they spend their leisure time.

You should draw a portrait or find a photo that would represent them too.

Step 4 – Scenarios

For each of your personas, imagine a positive or negative scenario in which each group might use a new interactive product or service. Keep the scenario to a single task and visualize each step that they would take in completing or not completing it. Write them down.

The task should reveal another list of potential content and functions for your service.

Step 5 – Integrate

Add together the two lists of content and functions from Step 2 and Step 4. Remove any duplication.

Sort the list into categories and sub-categories that make sense to you: for example, home, work, music, film, personal, social and so on.

Design development

The information age is encouraging designers to find creative solutions that communicate, publish or utilize higher levels of data or information than ever before. This can be seen in precision-targeted online advertising, as well as in our ability to self-publish blogs and games that utilize user-created environments. Technology is moving so quickly that both traditional and new media are converging on our televisions, computers and phones; leading to a potentially bewildering situation for designers, who must ultimately understand how to translate client and user needs into interactive products or services. This requires imaginative ideas wedded to an analytical and structured approach, which should emerge in the crucial early design phases of an interactive project before visual design can begin.

More complexity in the media landscape has naturally led to increased specialization amongst designers, with new roles and job titles being created, such as **information architect**, **interaction designer**, **user experience designer** and **user interface designer**, amongst others. For creatives working in large agencies, these titles may be fairly commonplace, but for smaller studios and small projects, these roles may become rolled into one.

This chapter will begin with some conceptual thinking exercises before focusing on how information is gathered, processed and turned into a logical structure prior to navigation elements being added. Only at this stage can prototypes or 'wireframes' be created and tested. In addition, as animation and video are becoming gradually more prevalent in interactive design, the roles of storyboards and **animatics** will also be discussed. Finally, building prototypes would have limited value if designers and their clients were the only people to see them, so the critical development process of feedback and user testing will also be explained.

2

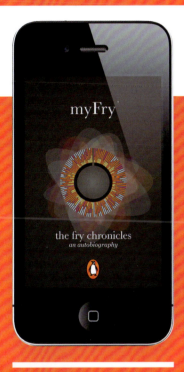

2.01–2.05 | myFry
myFry is an innovative eBook version of Stephen Fry's biography *The Fry Chronicles*, designed by Stefanie Posavec and developed by Dare. It uses an original visual index using key themes as tags within the text. These tags are divided into four important groupings: people, subjects, emotions and 'Fryisms'.

Conceptual thinking

Conceptual thinking is the ability to conceive ideas and select appropriate strategies for a given situation or problem. Conceptual thinking seeks to understand a situation and identify important underlying issues through the generation of problem-solving ideas that are critically evaluated. The following methods or techniques will help you to generate your own ideas. All of them can be undertaken individually, but many are better as group activities.

Brainstorming

Brainstorming is a creative exercise whereby new ideas are generated through spontaneous, intense and time-limited discussion. For group brainstorming sessions, a note-taker is normally appointed to write down new ideas and important notes on a flip chart or whiteboard. While the brainstorm's theme should be focused or broken down into a series of smaller topics, discussion should always be allowed to roam freely and develop naturally within given time constraints. The note-taker should be encouraged to write down all the ideas explored, no matter how inconsequential or abstract they might at first seem.

It is important to leave time at the end of the session to reflect on and evaluate the ideas generated. Rank their importance and organize them into related themes or topics where appropriate. Ask someone to type them up and distribute them for reflection. You may feel that you're in a position to give other individuals further tasks to complete based on the ideas generated.

Conceptual thinking exercises

Brain dumping	**Mind maps**
Brain storms	Laddering
Idea association	Random word
Making connections	Service prototyping
	Visualization

The exercises highlighted in bold are covered in this section.

2.06 | A gradual brainstorm
A Post-it note army by designer and illustrator Zara Gonzalez Hoang. Brainstorms are usually fast-paced group activities with lots of written thoughts but this collection of Post-it notes serves to remind us that they can be slower-paced, detailed and drawn activities too...

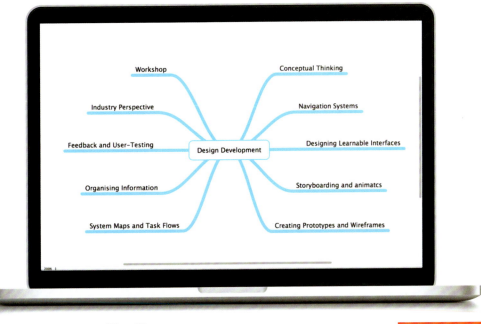

The mind map displayed on screen contains:

- Workshop
- Conceptual Thinking
- Industry Perspective
- Navigation Systems
- Feedback and User-Testing
- Design Development
- Designing Learnable Interfaces
- Organising Information
- Storyboarding and animatcs
- System Maps and Task Flows
- Creating Prototypes and Wireframes

2.07 | MindNode
MindNode is a useful digital tool for creating and sharing mind maps – but it is hard to beat pen and paper for recording ideas and connections quickly.

Mind maps

Mind maps are a graphical method of visualizing connections between words and ideas. They help designers to generate, visualize, order and classify ideas and information.

To create a mind map, write down the main topic in the centre of a sheet of paper. You may use words, symbols or images to help visualize connections that will radiate out from the centre. Use lines to show connections between words and images. Use different colours to distinguish between important themes and highlight keywords by underlining them or writing them in capital letters. Make sure that you consistently apply the styles you have chosen to use for organizing your mind map.

There are lots of digital mind-mapping tools also available, which are great for producing editable, organized and shareable maps; however, it is better to use these after your initial mind maps have been more quickly and easily developed on paper. Freemind and Mindnode are two such free tools that are available for Mac and Windows.

What if?

'What if?' is a lateral thinking method that generates new ideas by challenging the status quo. According to What If? Innovation Partners, in their book *Sticky Wisdom* (2002), questions can fall into four basic categories: re-expression, related world, revolution and random links.

Try re-expressing a design problem or issue using different words, or by expressing the problem in a different medium. You could, for example, simply draw it, or attempt to view it from another person's perspective: 'What if my organic grocery store was rebranded a "macrobiotic nutrition warehouse"?'

Sometimes, it's helpful to borrow ideas from a related field or situation. For example: 'What if the entrance to my grocery store was more like an airport departures lounge?'

Revolutionary questions can really be a great source of new ideas: 'What if my store was located on an organic farm and customers could select and watch their vegetables being freshly picked online?'

Introducing random links, associations, words or objects can be inspirational too: 'What if I gave my grocery store staff white gowns and called them "doctors"?'

2.08–2.09 | Solutionism
This idea generation card game developed by Mark Blythe asks two or more players to combine technologies, users, motives and problems in order to solve all of the world's problems and make everybody happy… Players rate each others' ideas for originality, plausibility and impact.

Making connections

Occasionally, designers and design students get the opportunity to set their own problems. Designing a new service or product for society relies on the complex interaction of many factors or requirements: focusing on a basic human need, identifying an audience, designing a compelling message (product or service), and using an appropriate medium. The message, product or service is often the most difficult factor to define so, by substituting it for a 'genre', we can start to generate new ideas.

Make connections between the different factors involved in the project that you are working on by selecting a category from each one and then combine them in order to generate a new idea for a product or service. For example: education + 25–34 yrs + platform game + smartphone = 'a casual game for language learning aimed at young professionals who have to collect words and assemble sentences in order to progress to the next level'. Alternatively, you may want to start off with fewer factors, for example human needs + mediums (see the table opposite).

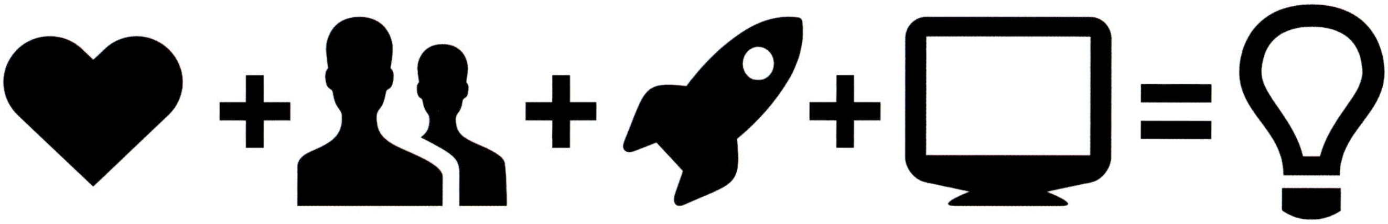

Make connections between the different factors involved in the project

Human need +	Target audience +	Genre +	Medium =	Ideas

Education
Knowledge

Family
Food
Kinship
Love
Security

Law
Crime
Security

Leisure
Entertainment
Exercise
Friendship

Religion
Science
Meaning of life

Work
Poverty
Social standing

Age
Under 10
11–14
15–17
18–24
25–34
35–48
49–65
65+

Sex
Male
Female

Origin/Race/Nationality
American
European
African
Asian
Australasian

Ability
Able-bodied
Disabled
Literate
Illiterate

Game Genres
Arcade
Action/Adventure
Mind games
Platform
Quiz/General knowledge
Reality
Simulation

Film Genres
Action
Adventure
Comedy
Crime
Documentary drama
Family
Fantasy
Film noir
Horror
Music
Musical
Mystery
Romance
Sci-Fi
Short
Thriller
War
Western

Media
Online
Offline
Interactive TV
Experiential
Ambient
Pervasive
Print
Convergent

Device
PC
Smartphone
Smart television
Tablet
Touch screen
Touch table
Kiosk
Game console

Peripherals
Digital camera
Webcam
Xbox connect
Wii controller
Arduino
GPS tracker
Dance mats
Infrared gun
Maracas

Organizing information

2.10 | CBH app
Cooperative Bulk
Handling (CBH) app
by Precedent: improving
harvesting efficiency
for grain growers in
Australia through
mobile technology.

As part of the consultation
process, Head of User
Experience and Strategy,
Dan Baker, created a
workshop for growers to
gain a solid understanding
of what they need and
want from a mobile app
or site.

When redeveloping an existing interactive product or service – for example, a website – it is essential to gain insights into the site's current capabilities and limitations; this will help the designer or specialist information architect to better understand a user's expectations of a website's content and functionality.

To achieve this aim, content gathering can be accomplished by utilizing a number of research methods, including interviewing current stakeholders, setting up focus groups and generating competitor analysis. An **information architect** may also want to perform more diagnostic assessments, such as user testing and analysis of web statistics, in order to discover common paths or clickstreams that users take when visiting a website. By taking a systematic approach to content gathering and assessments of usability, it is easier to ensure that the most appropriate content and functionality will be included in any redesign.

On the other hand, when time and access to current users or web statistics is not possible, an information architect may have to rely on fewer research methods, such as competitor analysis and the use of personas and scenarios. Certain research methods are also more problematic when developing a brand new product or service. For example, questionnaires and surveys have to be treated with caution while gathering information about potential content and function requirements; usability expert Jakob Nielsen sums up this situation neatly: 'To design an easy-to-use interface, pay attention to what users do, not what they say. Self-reported claims are unreliable, as are user speculations about future behaviour.'

2.11–2.14 | Scenarios and wireframes
The whiteboard was used as a way of graphically representing and sharing proposed content and functionality through a series of wireframes and related processes.

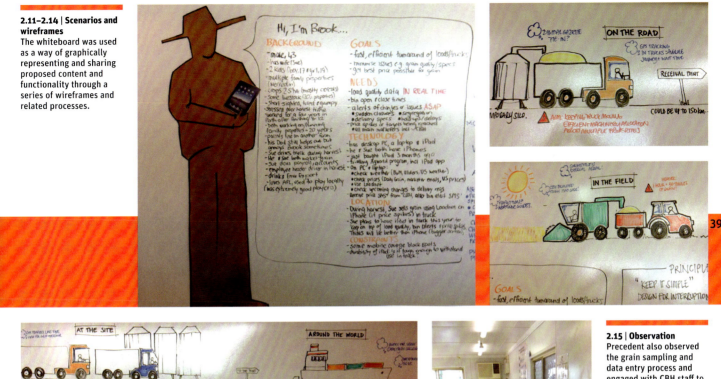

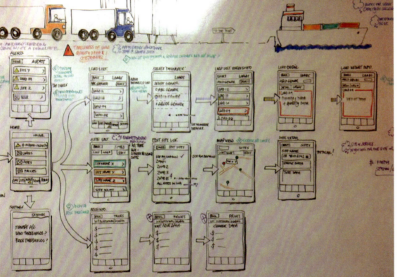

2.15 | Observation
Precedent also observed the grain sampling and data entry process and engaged with CBH staff to identify any gaps between app features members asked for and what the business could provide.

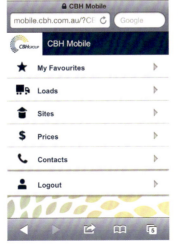

2.16–2.18 | CBH goes live
The mobile site went live in October 2012, just in time for the start of harvest, and is now being used by growers across Western Australia.

2.19 | Card sorting
Card sorting is a commonly used exercise used in interaction design and is not just restricted to web design. This multi-layered card sorting exercise by CIID Consulting was used during research interviews to map out the evolution and growth of community-driven organizations.

CIID Consulting met with various community leaders in the US to understand the process they had experienced while setting up a community-based initiative. Card sorting was undertaken during the interviews to gradually uncover different layers and to structure the conversation.

Sorting

Once a list of content has been gathered, it is time for the information architect to sort it into logical and meaningful groupings. The content may come in all kinds of forms, from text, images, video and sound, and may also be subdivided into rational hierarchies and chunks of information, such as headings, subheadings, sections and synopsis. Content should not be confused with a website or application's functionality; for example, search, download, register, login or media player. Both are required for the design site maps or user flows; however it is useful to list them discretely at this early sorting stage.

To help designers and information architects to categorize and arrange website content, a quick, inexpensive and robust method called 'card sorting' is often employed.

Card sorting

Card sorting is an activity that enables users to sort, group and organize the content of websites in ways that makes sense to them. Typically, numbered cards are labelled with categories, sub-categories and suggestions of content for participants to organize. The number of cards can vary from 20 to 100 with the activity ideally lasting no longer than an hour per participant. Participants are often encouraged to think out loud and add Post-it notes to cards with further ideas about content and functions. This additional feedback is important as it enables the information architect or designer to further understand the participants' reasoning and expectations for a website that would not necessarily be revealed during pure card sorting. The activity is repeated with a number of participants that represent the target audience for the product or service.

The first set of cards enabled the research participant (community leader) to map out a timeline and key milestones for the community's growth.

The second layer of cards was used to uncover stories that pinpointed challenges during the growth and significant moments that were drivers for progression.

The final set of cards helped the research participant to articulate key touchpoints that were crucial to the communities' success and so identify where they experienced personal reward during the growth process.

There are two methods of card sorting: open and closed. Open card sorting is generally used at the start of a website project when the information architect is interested in learning how participants would group content and label it. Closed card sorting uses predefined labels, and is often used in the latter stages of a project to validate ideas about content groupings. With either method, it is important to remember to take note of the card number orders and groupings, along with the comments made by participants.

If gathering participants together in the flesh is not possible because of time or geographical constraints, it can be useful to consider a number of online card sorting applications that are available. These applications vary in features; some support remote moderated sorting and many incorporate detailed data analysis. Whether using face-to-face participation or online applications, it is important to remember that the real value in card sorting is in the qualitative feedback provided by participants rather than in the quantitative data that may also be generated.

Card sorting software

Card Sort by UserZoom:
userzoom.com/products/card-sorting

MindCanvas:
themindcanvas.com/solutions/information-architecture/

OptimalSort:
optimalworkshop.com/optimalsort.htm

Simple Card Sort:
simplecardsort.com/

WebSort:
uxpunk.com/websort/

xSort:
xsortapp.com/

Site maps and task flows

The creation of site maps is an important task in the production of websites and interactive applications. It gives both the clients and the design and development teams a high-level view of the content structure, including the labelling and navigation systems.

2.22 | Visual Vocabulary
Jesse James Garrett's Visual Vocabulary shows some of the basic methods of depicting site maps and task flows.

Task flows differ from site maps as they represent the key steps and decisions for individual tasks, such as a login or search function for example, which may be performed without necessarily leaving the current page.

To help visualize site maps or task flows, a simple syntax is often used based on the Visual Vocabulary developed by user experience designer Jesse James Garrett.

When we dig a little deeper into the mapping of websites, it becomes clear that there are two basic kinds of page – static and dynamic – and that these characteristics affect how we map them. A static page often contains unique content that is updated infrequently, such as an 'about us' company web page. Dynamic pages are conversely empty 'containers' that are served with content when required.

News websites regularly use dynamic pages, whereby 'landing pages', such as the home page, are filled with time-sensitive chunks of content, which may include headlines, bylines and images. Each individual story can then be served to other relevant pages using as much of its chunked content as required. For example, a soccer-related story may appear on the home page, general sports landing page, soccer page, club page or even on a regional news page.

To provide detailed and understandable site maps and task flows, it is important to keep individual pages, content chunks or task flows accurately labelled with a logical numbering system so that clients, designers, developers and other stakeholders can follow and reference them.

Site mapping tools and resources

Adobe Illustrator
Axure RP Pro
iainstitute.org/tools/
jjg.net/ia/visvocab/
Microsoft Visio
OmniGraffle

Key

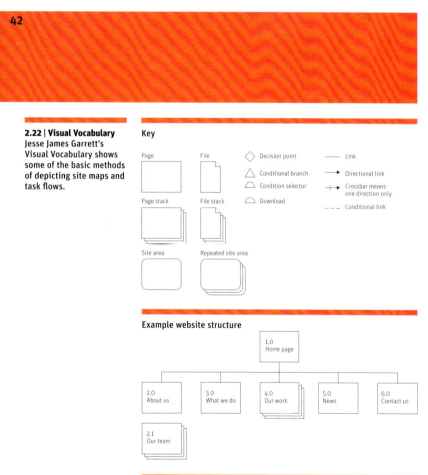

Example website structure

Example login and register sequence

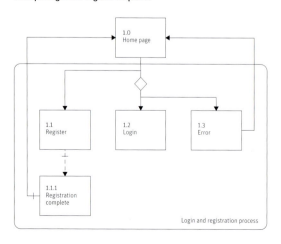

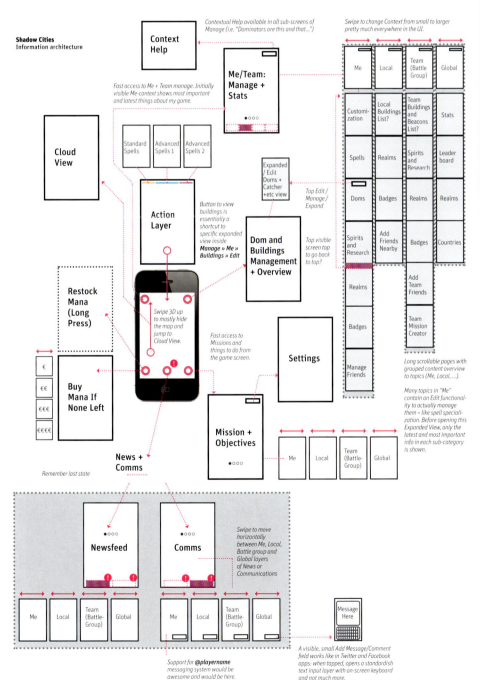

Shadow Cities
Information architecture

Made in **Nordkapp.**

2.23–2.25 | Shadow Cities
Nordkapp worked with games company Grey Area to redesign the user interface (UI) of the innovative Shadow Cities app game prior to its US launch. Nordkapp's new UI concept was based on long pages of grouped information, accessed from limited origin points on the screen with the use of swipe gestures to access sub-contexts. The new design utilized modern game and social media features, such as threading, missions, location awareness, notification, groups and events.

Navigation systems

Once the content has been decided upon, the organization of web pages agreed and the task flows of key functions identified, the designer needs to decide on an appropriate navigation system. Navigation systems help users to find useful content through browsing and searching. Navigation systems also help orientate the user through a sequence of web pages or tasks, and provide a logical hierarchy and order for content within an individual page.

In the section that follows, we will explore some of the features of navigation systems before then turning to explore the more conceptual considerations that might come into play when designing successful interfaces.

Websites, apps and other interactive products often employ both global and local navigation systems. 'Global navigation' describes buttons and links that are ever-present and usually sited in a consistent place, whereas 'local navigation' refers specifically to the section of content that you are in.

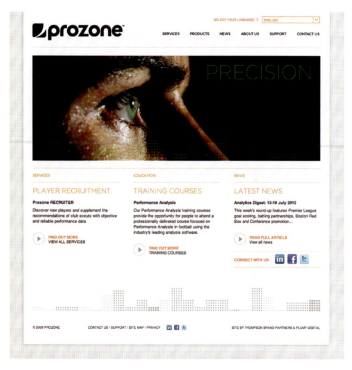

2.26 | Global navigation
This is the Prozone soccer analysis website designed by Plump Digital. The home page features a simple global navigation bar at the top of the page, giving universal access to top-level content areas such as services, support and contact us. To help users find the most important or popular content, there are quick links to the key services, education and news.

2.27 | Local navigation
To navigate within each content area, every page has its own 'local navigation' menu, featured here in the left-hand column. The main page content is in the middle column with the right-hand column used for additional content and related links. This is a classic web page layout and navigation system.

Browsing and searching aids

When using the Internet or on-demand television services, users invariably navigate by browsing or searching for the content. These two different forms of navigation have their own forms of navigation aids.

While browsing a website, we may use a number of browsing aids – from breadcrumb trails that help to show our current location, to site maps that give a bird's eye view of a website structure. We may also use site guides to help orientate ourselves within a particular section of a large website or sequential aids, such as 'Step 1 of 5', for specific sections.

Search interfaces are a common navigation method of locating the information we require, particularly when we may not know exactly what we are looking for or even where to look for it! Search engines, such as Google, use Boolean logic to help refine searches. Boolean logic uses 'operations' such as AND, OR, and NOT to establish the true and false values for a search – for example, 'Cats AND Dogs', 'Cats OR Dogs', 'Cats NOT Dogs'. Search engines also build queries that help to check our spelling or suggest alternative search terms, and can rank results based on how closely they match our search and the popularity of the results. When we select a result, our search can be further narrowed by location, time or similarity to a chosen result.

Navigation tips

Typically, most users use a combination of browsing and searching to find what they are looking for, so it is essential that multiple ways of navigating be provided for users. Remember: users performing searches will not all routinely enter your site from an established landing page, so clear labelling and positioning through the use of navigational tools, such as breadcrumb trails, is crucial.

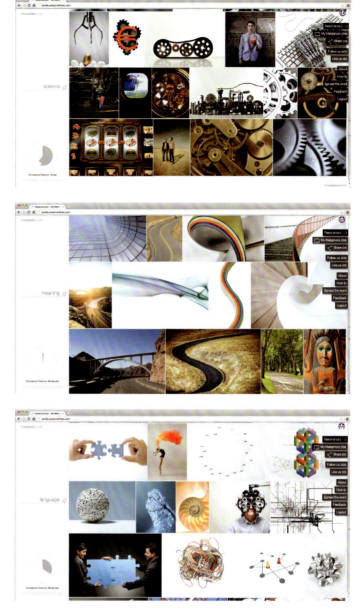

2.28–2.30 | Yossarianlives.com
Yossarianlives.com is a metaphorical search engine developed by Daniel Foster-Smith, J. Paul Neeley and Dr Katia Shutova. A metaphor is a type of comparison stated in the formula 'A is B', where the attributes of B are overlaid onto A. Take, for example, the notion that 'love is a river'. Love is not a river – the statement is patently false – but when we think about and understand the phrase metaphorically, we have a flash of insight.

The images show search results for the terms 'science', 'meaning' and 'language'. The 'Conceptual Distance' slider controls how closely related or disparate the metaphorical results are.

Designing learnable interfaces

2.31–2.36 | SoundPrism
A music app that makes complex harmonics easy to use through an intuitive user interface. Developed by Audanika with design consultancy Edenspiekermann, this innovative new app dispenses with old metaphors in favour of a completely fresh idiomatic design.

As the digital world is free from the constraints of physical reality, designers have the opportunity to invent new forms of user interface design that are fresh and fit for purpose rather than simply trying to mirror established design conventions. However, users in a digital space are impatient; the environment encourages interaction and speed, and users have typically become accustomed to engaging with interfaces that are familiar and intuitive rather than experimental ones that require new reasoning. But designing interfaces that are easy to learn is a difficult skill to master.

In this section, we will draw on the highly influential work of Donald Norman's classic book, *Emotional Design: Why We Love (or Hate) Everyday Things*, and Cooper, Reimann and Cronin's excellent tome, *About Face 3: The Essentials of Interaction Design*, to explain key concepts such as affordance, the limitations of metaphors and a general preference for idioms in the creation of successful user interfaces.

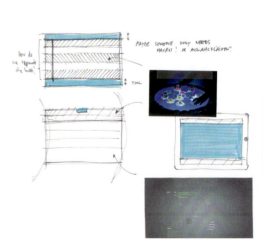

The power of attraction

Attractive interfaces are frequently perceived as more user-friendly. Donald Norman suggests that there are three basic motivations for completing a task in which our design is used: visceral, behavioural and reflective; they relate to how we feel, what we want to do and who we want to be. It is the user's visceral processing that gives a positive psychological and emotional response to the design. Therefore, a design that communicates attention to detail gives the user confidence that the product or service has been well designed. It builds immediate trust and a sense of pleasure from using it, resulting in increased creativity by the user. However, the design must also fulfil a user's functional expectations otherwise it will quickly lead to disappointment.

Affordance and the use of metaphors

Interfaces that give visible clues as to their use based on previous user experience are said to embody the concept of 'affordance'. Affordance is 'the perceived and actual properties of the thing, primarily those fundamental properties that determine just how the thing could possibly be used', according to Norman.

In the past, this has led designers to search for visual metaphors to help users navigate their way through an interactive application or website. Obvious examples are the desktop metaphor used in computer operating systems, and the ubiquitous shopping basket on e-commerce websites.

More recently, the search for attractive metaphors in app design has led to a recent trend in **skeuomorphic** design. A skeuomorph is the embellishment of a new design with the decorative form or aesthetic of an old design. Skeuomorphs are deliberately employed to make a new design appear familiar and attractive to the user.

Unfortunately, metaphors and skeuomorphic design can be very limiting. They rely on virtual processes having real-world equivalents, so opportunities for their successful use can be restrictive. Metaphors also scale poorly and are often culturally specific; short-term gains in the user's immediate understanding of an interface may lead to enduring restraints if the metaphor cannot be applied to explain more in-depth functionality.

Idioms

Idioms use natural language to help users learn how to use an interface without the need for metaphors or prior expertise. Idioms do not suffer from the inherent weaknesses of metaphors or the steep learning curves associated with many software packages because they rely on learning simple behaviours to perform tasks. 'All idioms must be learnt; good idioms need to be learnt only once' (Cooper et al, 2009).

Typically, idiomatic approaches guide users through a step-by-step approach, encouraging users to learn simple tasks and incrementally adding to their knowledge and expertise in using a new interface or system.

Metro, the design language created by Microsoft for its latest Windows 8 products, is a break from the previous icon-based operating systems and is an example of an idiomatic approach designed specifically for digital products.

2.37–2.41 | Madefire
A new interactive comic book publishing platform by Moving Brands, whereby custom-made navigation icons were required to be recognizable and intuitive from first use.

2.37 | Brand identity system
The full identity system for the Madefire brand, including the brand narrative, logos, wordmark, iconography, chiclet, and background textures.

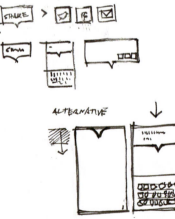

2.38 | Functionality development
Developing the 'sharing' functionality via seamless integration of social profiles was critical in order to foster and engage the powerful community that exists within the industry.

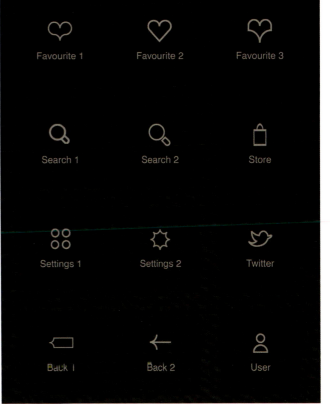

2.39 | Iconography development
The iconography style uses the geometric radii and sharp end points of the identity.

2.40 | Final iconography
All the assets in the identity system take cues from the logo using it as a thread to hold a very tight system together.

2.41 | App interface
The brand cues seen in the navigation buttons, background textures, loading animations and navbars are powerful reinforcements of the Madefire brand, but are subtle enough to ensure that the stories themselves are able to shine.

Creating prototypes and wireframes

The creation of prototypes lies at the intersection of three disciplines – information architecture, user-centred design and graphic design. Their purpose is to emulate and test the content, functionality and layout of an application or website.

Prototypes can take many forms, from simple paper-based sketches to polished digital prototypes, that are just a step away from final release. Prototyping is an iterative process that generally becomes more sophisticated with each passing project phase. The number and nature of prototypes depends on different factors – from time and budget to the expectations of the audience. A designer wanting to explain a method of interaction to a colleague may prototype with pen and paper as a level of shared understanding can be assumed. However, it is sometimes necessary to produce a highly polished conceptual prototype for the CEO of your client's organization in order to gain high-level buy-in and support for the project.

These examples illustrate the difference between wireframes and more realistic prototyping. Wireframes purposefully use simple outlined representations of screen elements, designed primarily to receive feedback on the functionality of an app or website, whereas realistic prototypes are designed to receive responses about aesthetic considerations and content.

A number of prototyping methods will be explained before offering further advice on choices.

Paper prototyping

The design of interactive projects can be tested using drawings of interfaces and webpage layouts, often called 'wireframes'. Two people are required to run the test – a note-taker and someone to act as the computer. When a participant presses a button or selects a feature on the wireframe, the person acting as the computer shows them where it will take them.

The advantages of paper prototyping are that it is quick, cheap to produce and redesigns can be implemented as soon as they are drawn!

Low-fidelity prototype

Once any initial problems have been ironed out through paper prototyping, a low-fidelity computer prototype can be created using Microsoft PowerPoint or a similar presentation tool that allows you to create a series of pages with interactive buttons and hotspots. This will give the participant a more authentic experience of the proposed design. At this stage, the testing is still largely focused on making sure that the right content and functions are displayed on the screen. A note-taker is required to record feedback.

High-fidelity prototype

This prototype may include real content and polished graphics. Specialist wireframing, prototyping or authoring software may be used; however, complex functions may not work and can be faked. This will give the designer more refined feedback on content, functions and aesthetics.

2.42–2.45 | Get Into Newcastle
Get Into Newcastle is a business and event listings website for the city of Newcastle, designed and developed by Komodo Digital. The images show the various stages of prototyping.

Top left: Site map.

Top right: Initial wireframe sketch.

Bottom left: Wireframe drawn using a popular wireframing stencil.

Bottom right: Digital wireframe.

50

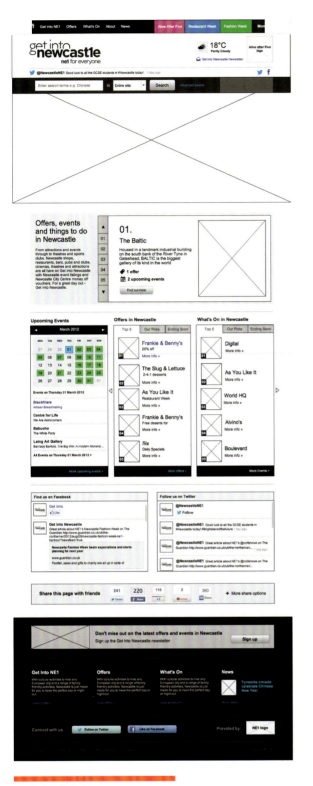

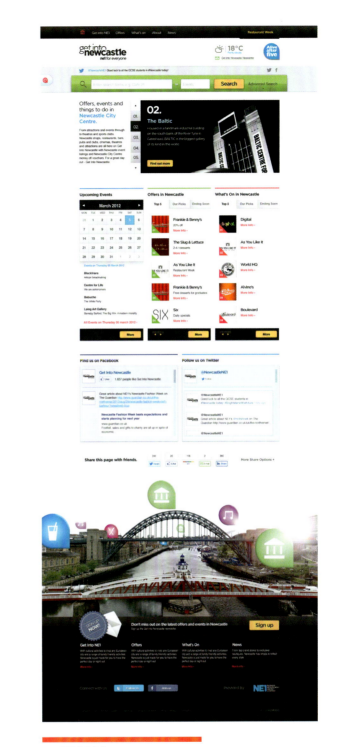

2.46 | Digital wireframe
Digital wireframes can be created in
graphics packages like Adobe Illustrator
or dedicated software such as Axure
or Balsamiq.

2.47 | High-fidelity prototype
Final graphics are often created in
Adobe Illustrator and/or Photoshop.

2.48–2.49 | SuomiTV

What will happen when television meets tablet computers? In 2010, SuomiTV and Nordkapp in Finland explored the future of television and created a concept to illustrate where they expected it to be in the near future.

These images show 4 stages in Nordkapp's design development process. The first two images (above and right) show an early low-fidelity paper prototyping stage.

2.50–2.55 | User behaviour concept

Wireframe sketches for the user interface behaviour.

Creating prototypes and wireframes → Storyboarding and animatics

2.56 | Final flow diagram
The final user interface scenario,
behaviours and the flow.

2.57–2.59 | High-fidelity prototypes
The final concept ready for
implementation and development.

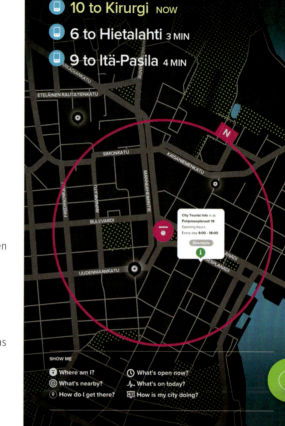

2.60–2.61 | Urbanflow
Urbanflow is a concept for urban screens situated in Helsinki made by Nordkapp and Urbanscale. These visuals were created in Adobe Illustrator and Photoshop.

The tools

The choice of digital prototyping tools used will partly rely on what is being evaluated, but it is also down to the personal preference of the designer or studio.

Many designers working in digital media prefer to use standard design packages, such as Adobe Illustrator and InDesign, to create wireframes. This is because the tools, such as Illustrator, can then be used to produce final screen layouts. When using these packages, or indeed many others, common graphics such as buttons, carousels and scroll bars are either created or downloaded to speed up the process. These visual elements are more commonly referred to as 'user interface' (UI) patterns.

Others prefer to use specialist wireframing tools such as Axure RP Pro, Balsamiq and Protoshare, which offer more features such as interactive functionality, annotation and discussion tools.

For more polished prototypes assessed in more authentic situations, high quality visual screens can be created in graphics packages, such as Adobe Photoshop, and authored using Adobe Dreamweaver or WordPress for web projects. For apps, software such as Proto.io or App in Seconds provide more realistic prototypes.

Video prototyping

Video prototyping has become a very powerful prototyping tool for designers to use throughout the development phase. Video is often used to produce low-fidelity prototypes for idea sharing and is particularly useful as a means of recoding development and communicating when team members may be working in different offices and locations. Highly polished video prototypes that use animation and post-production effects to make ideas appear more realistic are widely used to promote ideas and receive buy-in from clients or potential investors, sometimes before any genuine design or development work has actually been done.

Creating prototypes and wireframes → Storyboarding and animatics

2.62–2.68 | Stills from the Urbanflow video
A high-fidelity prototype was created to explain the potential for an interactive city information system. Project website: *helsinki. urbanflow.io/*

55

Assessing more polished prototypes

Wireframing tools	App prototyping tools	UI patterns
Adobe Illustrator	*appinseconds.com*	*graffletopia.com*
Adobe InDesign	*balsamiq.com*	*konigi.com*
axure.com	*invisionapp.com*	*patternry.com*
balsamiq.com	*justinmind.com*	*patterntap.com*
Microsoft PowerPoint	*popapp.in*	ui-pattterns.com
protoshare.com	*proto.io*	*welie.com*

Storyboarding and animatics

Storyboards are a highly effective way to communicate ideas and tell stories for a wide range of design applications – from television *title sequences* to interactive projects. They are used primarily as a pre-production activity, allowing designers to explain their ideas for client approval, and for creative teams to reach a mutual understanding before an animation, video or user experience is produced.

Storyboards

Storyboards can be created with pen and paper or by using digital software, or, more often than not, a combination of both. The level of detail, like prototyping, will very much depend on what needs to be communicated to whom. Basic sketches will suffice for sharing ideas, but more in-depth drawings or paintings will be required to convey the detail of actual scenes, lighting and moods.

Before drawing a storyboard, it is important to have a script or a thorough brief to work from. At this stage, a list of key moments can be written down to form the basis for your boards. Visuals may only form part of the narrative, as dialogue, sound effects and music could also help tell the story. To convey this, explanatory notes, dialogue and timings should also accompany each storyboard image. If the sequence uses live action, additional information, such as the location and time of day, should be included too.

To integrate all this information, paper-based templates can be used, although hand-drawn sketches and paintings are usually scanned and added to digital templates produced in Adobe Illustrator or InDesign. These files can then be more easily shared digitally with clients and creative teams.

It is important to remember that a storyboard is only a means of communicating ideas, so many versions may need to be produced before a final version is agreed upon. A good storyboard will clarify intentions and save time and money, so getting it right is important.

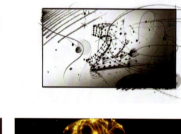

2.69–2.76 | Storyboards
Drawn storyboards by Maylin Gouldie/Red Bee for a BBC2 identity, communicate the energy and excitement required for the final visuals.

Animatics

Animatics are storyboard images or more polished static visuals sequenced in a video-editing package along with sample music to give a better sense of timing and creative intention. They are the next logical step in the process of designing a narrative sequence and allow both the client and creative team a further opportunity to judge an idea before committing to the costly production phase of a project. While animatics naturally follow storyboards, they may be sidestepped or replace storyboards depending on the agreed phases of a project.

2.77–2.88 | Previz
Uber Digital was commissioned by Eastman to create an animation that highlights both the functional and emotional attributes of Eastman Tritan™ copolyester material in the Dunkfish, a tea-infuser created by Zeewok. This animatic, also known as a 'previz' (previsualization), was produced to help the client get a better feel for the movement, pace and information presented in the intended animation. It formed one part of a full design process that also included storyboarding, modelling, colour and sound.

2.89–2.91 | Final animation
The final animation was featured on EastmanInnovationLab.com and was produced in mp4, wmv, iPad and iPhone formats for use across a range of digital media.

Feedback and user-testing

Feedback on your design can start as soon as you've developed your first prototype and should continue in a cycle of development and feedback until your project is complete. Feedback can take many forms, from a simple discussion between designer and client through to more complex methods involving focus groups and even surveys. User-testing is a form of feedback employed for products and services that require users to perform certain tasks to discover where they encounter difficulties, for example, the programming of a microwave oven or the navigation of a website. Three forms of prototyping and two methods of testing will be discussed, which can be combined to help you assess your designs.

Conducting a simple user test

For a designer working on a small commercial project with a limited budget, extensive user testing may be too time-consuming or cost prohibitive. However, simple user tests can be conducted with as little as five to six participants. Give each participant a list of tasks to perform using your prototype and observe them one at a time. Document your observations in a notepad, particularly those instances where participants become confused or run into problems. Encourage participants to vocalize their actions and thought processes so that you can understand the thinking behind their decisions. You can also video record the tests if you want to re-watch them later.

Conducting a more sophisticated heuristic evaluation

Heuristic evaluation uses a small group of participants known as 'evaluators' to uncover usability issues. It differs from the simple user test because the evaluator records the observations instead of an independent observer. Evaluators are often experienced users of similar products who determine their own tasks and assess them against a set of ten recognized usability principles. The more 'evaluators' that assess the design, the more usability problems will be discovered. Again, five to six evaluators would provide a solid basic assessment.

2.92–2.94 | The Ableton website
Edenspiekermann were asked to create a website to bring the new Ableton brand to life. Together with Ableton's web team, they co-created the new site using agile methodologies. As an integrated team of designers and developers, they were able to iterate on the most important sections of the website, such as the product tours and shop, incorporating feedback from users and stakeholders in weekly reviews.

Ten usability principles

The following ten principles are based on Jakob Nielsen's Ten Usability Heuristics and should be used to heuristically evaluate a design.

1

Design with elegant simplicity
Your design should be attractive yet minimal. The user should be able to select functions and access content without being distracted by overly complex and superfluous design.

2

Use familiar language and conventions
Your design should use verbal and visual language, and conventions that are both familiar and reassuring for the user group. User experience should be intuitive, encouraged by a logical ordering of information and processes.

3

Be consistent
Your design should be consistent in the language and conventions that it uses. The greater the similarity and consistency there is with other designs, the quicker and easier it will be for users to become familiar with your design.

4

Be visible
Your design should make actions, objects and options constantly visible, so reducing the need for users to have to memorize them. A 'Help' feature should always be available, too.

5

Provide visible feedback
Your design should always keep users informed about what's happening through timely and appropriate feedback.

6

Provide control
Your design should give the user complete functional control, with the ability to cancel actions, and provide a simple exit function if the user decides not to continue with a process.

7

Provide shortcuts
Your design should provide shortcuts for expert users, which won't confuse or distract novice users. Where possible, allow users to customize frequent actions.

8

Prevent errors
Your design should try to eliminate the chance of a user making errors; or at the very least, present the user with a confirmation screen asking them to verify their actions and so make them think twice about their choices.

9

Report errors
Your design should report errors in a clear and comprehensible language, so helping the user to understand why and how the error has occurred and what they need to do to rectify the situation.

10

Provide help
Your design should be an intuitive process for users and, wherever possible, should obviate the need for them to read a manual in order to understand how to navigate it. When help is required, it should be searchable, pertinent and simple to follow.

Industry perspective:
Campbell Orme, Moving Brands

Client
Hitachi

Brief
To design the user-facing experience of new innovative interactive software, which allowed for remote collaboration, using a projected, gesture-based interface.

Agency
Moving Brands

Solution
Moving Brands created detailed user journeys, logic flows, user interaction guidelines and a full user interface, for implementation and build by Hitachi's Tokyo-based development team.

Interview with Campbell Orme,
Design Director, Moving Brands
Campbell has worked in design and direction roles for a number of international design agencies including Moving Brands, Imagination, BERG and Pentagram. Campbell's specialism is interactive projects, which include online, interactive installations, software applications and custom, hardware-specific software.

2.96 | UX pattern mapping
Key gestures were mapped to the user interface to ensure that there was an appropriate and consistent use of language.

2.97 | Key gesture and interface taxonomies
Mapped key gesture and interface taxonomies were employed to ensure that they were appropriate for context of use.

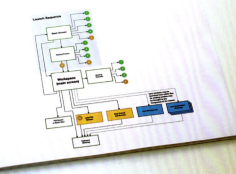

2.98 | UX simplification
Extensive user flows mapped the logic of navigating the software. This systematic approach was necessary to reduce the complexity of the UX, wherever possible.

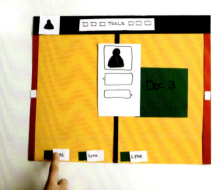

2.99 | Quick paper prototyping
Prototyping does not have to be polished! Paper prototyping allowed for quick exploration and iteration of the UX.

2.100 | Optimizing assets
The scale and relatively low resolution of the projected interface meant that assets had to be optimized for the software.

2.101 | Exploring key behaviours and interactions
Prototyping included Processing applications, which allowed for exploring key behaviours and interactions on the hardware itself.

After your initial briefing, how did you set about structuring the whole project?

There were a number of clear phases in the project, which spanned: requirements gathering, feasibility, information architecture, user flows, user experience (UX) and user interface design (UI).

Can you describe the 'requirements gathering' phase?

Some of the criteria that we look to summarize here are: 'How do we succinctly describe the perceived outcome?'; 'What is its purpose and who is it for?'; and 'What will the target user group actually require of it?' This last question is especially important as it's one of the means of validation that we use for ascertaining whether the brief has been met.

What research methods did you use to achieve this?

Alongside current trend and market analysis, we worked with our client to get under the skin of what were deemed to be the core features of the software. Equally, as the end product was going to be targeted to a specific audience type – corporate, education and civic environments – we looked at what parallel user-case scenarios, away from technology, were relevant.

Could you explain the 'feasibility' phase?

What we needed to know from the outset was whether our proposals were technically achievable, for fear of winding up with a design that couldn't be realized. As there were third-party technologies being employed for some of the messaging and network feature – each with their own API nuances – we had to be aware of how these functioned.

What happened next?

The next stage looks at the information architecture: the overall structure of the software. This often uses user journeys and flows, to ensure the given steps within a task are efficient and clear. This in turn leads into UX – page layouts and frames – and then eventually into the UI phase. These phases are never neat and frequently overlap, as we find issues that require us to revisit earlier phases. What this all means is that the fidelity and definition of the end product is continually being refined as the project progresses.

Industry perspective:
Campbell Orme, Moving Brands

2.102 | UI toolkit
Alongside the information architecture and user experience, and a full, pixel-perfect UI toolkit was created for development, optimized for projection and viewing distance.

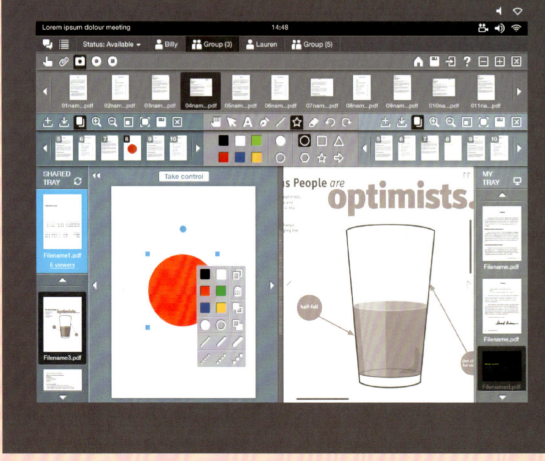

63

What form do user journeys take?

These are often a combination of paper prototypes, video demonstrations, or clickable interactives. These all have their individual strengths; for example, we find clickable demos are very useful for website wireframes, where we deliberately package up something that looks very rough to give the client a sense of walking through the end product without them fixating on its aesthetic appearance.

What is the purpose of video prototypes?

It depends on who they're for. For the development team, they might be rough-and-ready stories to discuss how to navigate the product – to demonstrate a sequence that's hard to convey on paper. For the client's CEO, it may have to look very real, with a level of polish or realism that serves to get top-level buy-in for the project.

You're developing a new product, so was it important to use familiar visual metaphors for the user interface?

As designers and developers, it's preferable to lean on metaphors and tropes that are familiar to both end users and us. However, we quickly found that some of these weren't applicable for this project. Designing a gesture-based interface for a six-feet-wide screen presents new design problems, as, for example, people's height and size come into play. You can't use a traditional top-down menu if some people may have trouble reaching it. Similarly, you can't automatically decide on a menu on the left or right of the screen without acknowledging a left- or right-hand bias.

How do you visually research a project?

One of the first things we do is try and understand the client's visual tone of voice. How do they represent themselves in the real world? Next, we have to assess whether what we are doing has to sit alongside it, or has to work completely within it, or indeed has to be distinct.

What visual methods of research do you use?

We still use moodboards however they manifest themselves, and we often create mood films with sound and moving image that try to reflect the client's tone of voice. They are not a means to an end in themselves, but they are effective for setting a project's tone at an early stage, in a format that is self-presenting and easily shared.

Did you undertake a formal user-testing?

On occasion, we might engage a third-party user-testing company to organize formal assessments and focus groups within our target audience, but for confidentiality reasons this was less viable with this project. However, we did a lot of user-testing with the client's development partner – the teams at Moving Brands and Hitachi's teams in Japan – and with people in our studio not directly involved with the project.

Workshop II:
The Cube

The following workshop is intended to give you practice at designing a system flow and wireframe interface. The exercise could last from two hours to a whole day depending on the level of detail and complexity you wish to include.

Background

The Burj Khalifa in Dubai is the tallest building in the world with its spire reaching almost half a mile into the sky (2,720 feet/830 metres). The building has 160 floors with the highest nightclub in the world on the 144th floor. It has the fastest elevators in the world travelling at 40 mph (64 kph) or 60 feet (18 metres) per second.

'The Cube' is an imaginary new apartment block in Dubai with 1,600 apartments. The four sides of the building each contain 400 apartments arranged in a 20x20 grid. Each apartment is directly accessible by eight revolutionary multi-directional elevators that can move horizontally and vertically around all four sides of the building. In addition to the 20 floors of living accommodation, the ground floor contains a lobby area and the 21st floor a leisure complex, making 22 floors in total.

The brief

Your brief is to design the interface for The Cube's elevator control system. Think about the basic functions of selecting an apartment, hold open or close door, and help/emergency. Visualize how to display important information; for example, current floor or apartment and direction of travel. You may want to consider other features the lift may have to keep the users calm or entertained.

2.104 | Understanding users
Identify fictitious users and understand their potential needs.

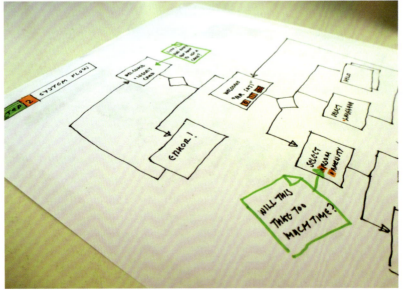

2.105 | System flow
Create flow diagrams to demonstrate the elevator's basic functionality.

Adding further complexity

You might want to imagine what amenities will be on the ground or top floor and how a user might quickly select them; for example, cafés, restaurants, crèche, nightclub, swimming pool, gyms or even squash courts.

Dubai is an international destination attracting many nationalities. A new and complex lift system would require a help feature in numerous languages, but how would this work?

Security might also be an issue: how would someone feel about accessing a public lift that opens directly into a private apartment? Or even prevent an intruder from gaining access?

Finally, what would happen if there was an elevator already outside your chosen apartment? Or what if two people in different elevators both chose to go to the same apartment or hotel amenity?

Principles of interaction

Consider the following principles of interaction when thinking about your design:

Visibility – make sure the user can see and understand the most important options available to him or her.

Predictability – do not move information and interactive features about for the sake of it – it should be predictable. You want the user to spend time looking at information and not wondering how to make something work!

Feedback – if an interactive feature is used or selected, give the user feedback to show that it has worked; for example, a button lights up or they hear a click.

Learnability – a good interface helps the user remember how to use it so that they do not have to relearn it every time.

Consistency – an interface should ideally share basic working principles with other devices. For example, the buttons to play, stop, pause, fast forward and rewind are universal and are very similar on a CD player, a video recorder, YouTube and iTunes. If you introduce a new method of interaction, it should be because it is better, not just different.

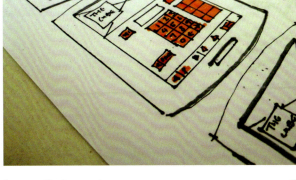

Step 1 – Understand

Take time to think about the needs of potential users – for example, whether they are young or old, apartment owners or visitors, etc. – and also identify potential issues. Make a list of these potential needs and issues.

Step 2 – System flow

Create a system flow for the elevator's basic functions and work out what buttons and display information will be required to use them.

Step 3 – Wireframe

Design a wireframe interface for your elevator. Consider how user feedback on selection will be given, such as a glowing button, graphic displayed on a screen, audio confirmation or a combination of them all.

2.106 | Wireframes
Create simple drawn wireframes to illustrate the user interface.

Colour and image

Colour and image are the two most important visual elements at a designer's disposal. These elements are often used intuitively and mark out those fortunate people who are visually gifted from those who are not. For this reason, explaining a colour choice or image use can seem difficult at first or hard to defend for inexperienced designers. This chapter will attempt to make sense of our design decision-making by explaining relevant theory and technical considerations, and offering practical advice on both colour and image use.

Colour psychology and its specific digital importance will be highlighted before covering how colours are created and applied on both television and the Web. In a similar flow, key semiotic theory will be introduced to illustrate how digital images are 'encoded' and 'decoded' before technical considerations for digital media uses are explained. The use of photo libraries and related visual resources will be detailed as part of a designer's toolbox.

3

3.01–3.05 | Generative design
Onformative in co-operation with Interbrand created a tool for the automatic image generation of molecule graphic imagery for pharmaceutical company Actelion.

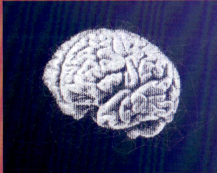

Colour meaning and psychology

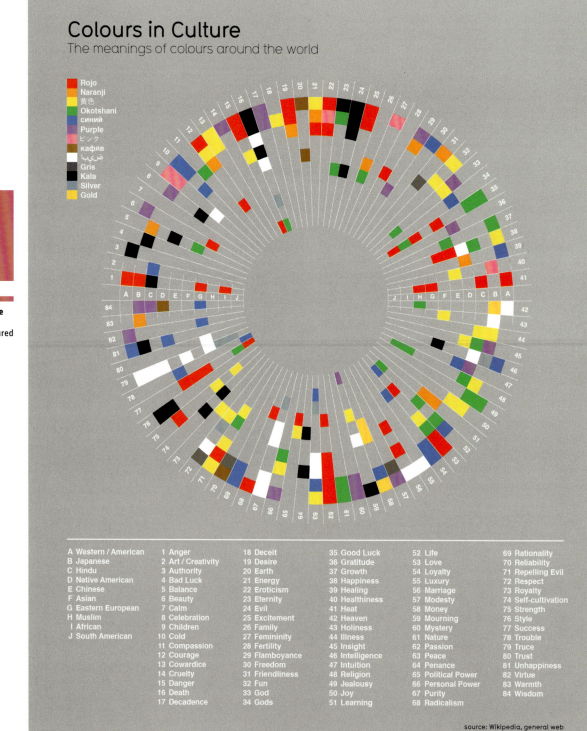

Colours in Culture
The meanings of colours around the world

Legend:
- Rojo
- Naranji
- 黄色
- Okotshani
- синий
- Purple
- ピンク
- кафяв
- ضيب
- Gris
- Kala
- Silver
- Gold

A Western / American	1 Anger	18 Deceit
B Japanese	2 Art / Creativity	19 Desire
C Hindu	3 Authority	20 Earth
D Native American	4 Bad Luck	21 Energy
E Chinese	5 Balance	22 Eroticism
F Asian	6 Beauty	23 Eternity
G Eastern European	7 Calm	24 Evil
H Muslim	8 Celebration	25 Excitement
I African	9 Children	26 Family
J South American	10 Cold	27 Femininity
	11 Compassion	28 Fertility
	12 Courage	29 Flamboyance
	13 Cowardice	30 Freedom
	14 Cruelty	31 Friendliness
	15 Danger	32 Fun
	16 Death	33 God
	17 Decadence	34 Gods

35 Good Luck	52 Life	69 Rationality
36 Gratitude	53 Love	70 Reliability
37 Growth	54 Loyalty	71 Repelling Evil
38 Happiness	55 Luxury	72 Respect
39 Healing	56 Marriage	73 Royalty
40 Healthiness	57 Modesty	74 Self-cultivation
41 Heat	58 Money	75 Strength
42 Heaven	59 Mourning	76 Style
43 Holiness	60 Mystery	77 Success
44 Illness	61 Nature	78 Trouble
45 Insight	62 Passion	79 Truce
46 Intelligence	63 Peace	80 Trust
47 Intuition	64 Penance	81 Unhappiness
48 Religion	65 Political Power	82 Virtue
49 Jealousy	66 Personal Power	83 Warmth
50 Joy	67 Purity	84 Wisdom
51 Learning	68 Radicalism	

source: Wikipedia, general web

3.06 | Colours in Culture
'Colours in Culture' by David McCandless featured in his book *Information Is Beautiful* (2010).

68

Colours conjure powerful emotions in all of us, from radiant reds and cool blues through to sombre greys and autumnal hues. We derive meaning from colour in numerous ways, from its associations with nature to man-made links with our history and culture. For these reasons, there are both universal perceptions of colour – for example, orange means warm and green means healthy – as well as culturally specific associations – black represents death in western societies in contrast to China where white is used.

Sometimes colours are chosen arbitrarily and gain historical significance. Have you ever wondered why Sir Tim Berners-Lee chose the colour blue for hyperlinks when red would arguably have been a more logical choice for an interactive element?

While there are many universally accepted colour associations, colours often have different meanings dependent on the context in which they are used: a red sports car, a red dress, a red warning sign, a red Coca-Cola can, a red Santa Claus suit…

Digital designs for websites, smartphone apps and video games are often required to reach a global rather than local audience so understanding how colours may be interpreted is very important. The chart opposite illustrates how colour is perceived by various nationalities and cultures.

3.07–3.08 | Barbour website
The Barbour website, designed by Nation, reflects both the cultural heritage and natural muted colours associated with the brand.

Colour in technical detail

3.09–3.12 | CX identity
CX identity by Moving Brands developed
through many iterations of colour,
typography and image experimentation.

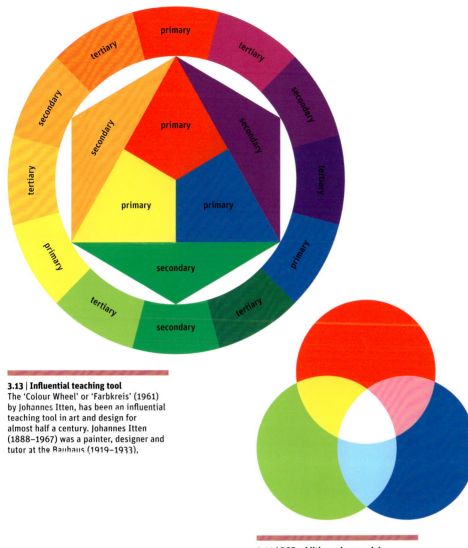

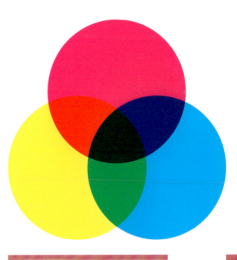

3.15 | CMYK subtractive colour model
Used for commercial printing.

3.13 | Influential teaching tool
The 'Colour Wheel' or 'Farbkreis' (1961) by Johannes Itten, has been an influential teaching tool in art and design for almost half a century. Johannes Itten (1888–1967) was a painter, designer and tutor at the Bauhaus (1919–1933).

3.14 | RGB additive colour model
Used for the display of on-screen images.

Our basic model of colour, also known as the 'artist's model', is based on the primary colours of red, yellow and blue. From these primary colours, all other colours can be mixed. Secondary colours are created from mixing two primary colours in equal measure. Mixing a primary and secondary colour in equal measure further creates tertiary colours. With this basic palette, it is easy to create colour schemes for our designs.

Unlike the artist's model, designers use two alternative colour models with different primaries to create colour: RGB (red, green, blue) and CMYK (cyan, magenta, yellow and key black). These two models are used because red, yellow and blue cannot be used successfully to create adequate colour ranges on screen using light or in commercial printing using pigment.

RGB is known as an additive system because the more colour that is added, the lighter and brighter the final colour becomes. CMYK is a subtractive system because the more colour that is mixed, the darker the final colour appears. A key colour of black is required to supplement the cyan, magenta and yellow because when mixed together they cannot produce a true black on their own. Naturally, RGB is the system we use for screen-based design whereas CMYK is used in print publishing.

While digital images use RGB channels of colour, it is often easier to work with a Hue, Saturation and Brightness (HSB) colour model to select RGB colour. With this system, you can choose the Hue (pure component of colour), and then adjust its Saturation (intensity) and Brightness according to your need.

Working with colour

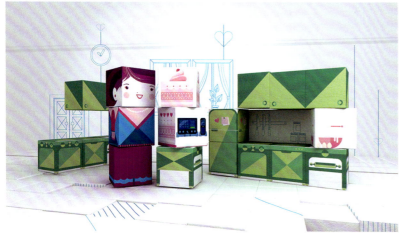

3.16–3.17 | Connected Home
This is Telstra's 'Connected Home' commercial by Psyop.
This charming stop-motion effect computer animation
uses a building block visual concept to drive the
commercial's 'connected theme'. This animation uses
a white background, which is unusual on television.
Large areas of flat bright or saturated colours have to
be carefully filtered to avoid broadcasting images with
too much contrast. For this reason, pure white or black
are avoided as they are 'unsafe' and may cause image
distortion on television.

Colour for television

The human eye can only see a small proportion of the sun's
rays – what we term as light – and within this colour range
or 'gamut', our colour systems and devices are even more
limited. Have you ever looked at the iridescent colour of
flowers and wondered why they are never as vivid in print
or on television? The answer is that our man-made colour
models cannot replicate their depth of hue or saturation.

The RGB system is made up of 256 shades of each colour
(values 0–255) that when combined together create over
16 million different shades of colour. Computer monitors
can recreate this spectrum; however, other devices, such
as televisions, are more limited by the broadcast standards
used. For example, the PAL broadcast standard used widely
in Europe cannot display very saturated or pure colours and
limits the luminance range to 16–235. NTSC, the standard
in North America, is even more restrictive. Colours used
outside this range would distort the TV image, as will high
contrasting areas of flat colour.

Luminance is not the only restriction. Single horizontal
lines and high contrasting patterns of colour, for example,
dog-tooth patterns, should also be avoided because they
will appear to flicker. Television broadcasts interlace
images to your TV set, which means that the odd lines
of the image then the even lines are displayed in quick
succession, therefore any single pixel width lines or details
will appear then disappear or flicker.

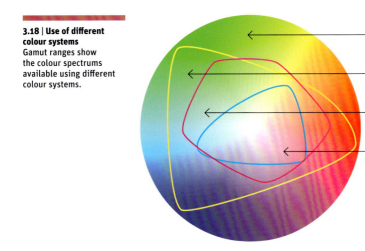

3.18 | Use of different colour systems
Gamut ranges show the colour spectrums available using different colour systems.

Visible colour gamut

RGB colour gamut

Pantone colour gamut

CMYK colour gamut

3.19 | TV safe colours
This diagram shows how the brightest colours have to be filtered out before broadcast.

Colour for the Web

Colour schemes for websites generally reflect their intended design aspirations or brand values. However, care needs to be taken to design colour schemes that maximize legibility and intuitive navigation. Black body text on a white background gives the greatest contrast for legibility, although a subtle off-white shade with dark tones for text may provide a more aesthetically pleasing choice while still maintaining legibility. While working with colour, it is often easier to work with a more limited range of colour to begin with to maintain control over legibility and colour consistency of interactive and non-interactive elements. When choosing colours for all types of link, it's often wise to choose a monochromatic range with perhaps a complementary colour for the active state. Never make them all the same colour as this will result in the user not receiving visual feedback on whether they have selected or previously visited a page.

Note: Web colours are often expressed in hexadecimal values. Hexadecimal numbers (base 16) are commonly used in computing because they translate directly into binary. Each RGB colour is represented by two numbers or letters, so pure red (RGB 255,0,0) is #ff0000 in hex.

Finally, the beauty of the Web is that it can customize and adapt content instantly for individual needs. This allows users with accessibility issues, such as colour blindness, the opportunity to view pages that are designed to overcome their legibility issue. Colour blindness affects about 12% of males of European origin and 0.5% of women. Ideally, a designer should check their intended colour palettes with a number of online tools; however, one technical solution is to create separate Cascading Style Sheets (CSS) for different visual impairments. CSS are tiny files that contain the visual styling elements, for example, typographic details and colours used, as well as layout positions. Style sheets are more commonly used to differentiate the layout and styling requirements between desktop, smartphone and tablet devices.

3.20–3.22 | Web page colour schemes
These examples from the BBC show how a web page's colour schemes need to change for users with different visual impairments.

Using colour systems

Colour can both harmonize and organize graphic elements and information. Using colours based on a working knowledge of the colour wheel will provide your design with balance, harmony and organization. The basic colour schemes are explained below.

Monochromatic schemes are created by taking a single colour and adding neutral colours to create shades. Monochromatic schemes are harmonious and easy on the eye, but are weaker at highlighting areas of interest.

Analogous schemes typically use colours that are adjacent in the colour wheel. Analogous schemes are harmonious in the same way as monochromatic, but they have the benefit of being able to accent or highlight areas of interest.

Complementary schemes use pairs of colour that are opposite each other in the colour wheel. They are good for highlighting features, and work best when one colour

is more dominant than the other where the less dominant colour is used as the accent colour.

Split complementary schemes are made from three colours. Choose a colour then select colours from either side of its natural complementary colour. Split commentary schemes create impact, but are often hard to balance.

Triadic schemes are created by choosing three colours that are equidistant on the colour wheel. As with split complementary, triadic schemes are dynamic, but difficult to balance, and often work best when one colour is dominant.

Adjacent colours

Although colour values can be set, their appearance will change depending on their surroundings, in particular adjacent colours. In general, colours appear brighter on dark backgrounds and are more muted when placed next to a colour of a similar hue.

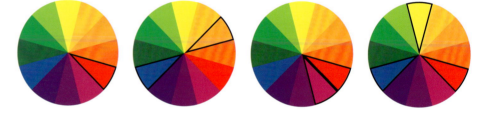

3.23 | Colour harmonies
From left to right: monochromatic, complementary, analogous, split and triadic schemes.

3.24 | colorschemedesigner.com
Designed by Petr Staníček.
colorschemedesigner.com

3.25 | Colour guide
This window panel is a feature of Adobe Illustrator.

Colour scheme creation

In Adobe Illustrator, you can use the 'Colour Guide' panel (accessible from the Window menu) to help you find colour schemes based on your current fill colour. Alternatively, use online resources to find or create colour schemes:

colorschemedesigner.com

colorsontheweb.com

colourlovers.com

kuler.adobe.com

pictaculous.com

web.colorotate.org

3.26–3.27 | The Tommy portfolio site
Creative agency Tommy has used a
retro colour scheme to complement its
hand-rendered logotype, which together
create a nostalgic 1970s motoring aesthetic.

Encoding and decoding images

When we create or select images, our choices are far more sophisticated than we might at first imagine. How do we know that the viewer or 'reader' will share our understanding of the image, or receive them in the way we intended?

Semiotics may hold the answer. This is the study of signs and symbols, their use and interpretation. The subject was developed independently by Ferdinand de Saussure, a Swiss linguistics professor, and an American philosopher, Charles Peirce, at the turn of the twentieth century. The meaning of any image or sign lays in the sign itself, how it is organized and the context in which it appears. This is incredibly important for design and has particular resonance for interactive design, as the reader may not share our language or culture, and we may have little control over the time, place or context in which an image is viewed.

As with colour, the inspiration for the signs we create comes from two basic sources: nature and culture. We might use a green apple from nature to represent health, yet the Red Cross – the international symbol for humanitarian aid – is a cultural reference: it is the reversed colours of the Swiss flag and denotes the origin of its founder Henry Dunant and the Geneva Convention in 1864 that established it.

The following paragraphs explain some very basic concepts of semiotics, enough to help us start to question our choice of image. For further reading, please refer to David Crow's *Visible Signs: An Introduction to Semiotics in the Visuals Arts* (2010) or Sean Hall's *This Means This, This Means That: A User's Guide to Semiotics* (2012).

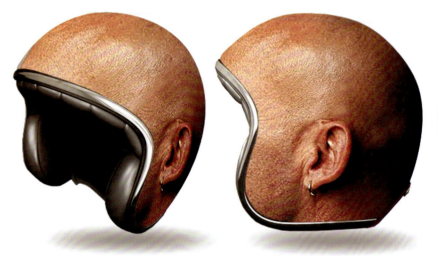

3.28 | UDesign Studio
This creative helmet by Igor Mitin signifies conflicting visual messages to us: it is a crash helmet, therefore it is safe – and yet the bald head surface image indicates a certain fragility in the context of motorcycling, which makes the combination both unusual and dangerously exhilarating.

Icons are signs commonly used to
create meaning. Some are literal
representations, such as a paintbrush;
others are metaphorical or analogous.

Literalness, analogies and metaphors

Signs are literal, analogical or metaphorical and help us to
derive meaning. Literal signs represent meaning exactly:
a paintbrush icon in Adobe Photoshop signifies that we can
paint with a brush, whereas the blur tool represented by a
water droplet is an analogy because it is 'like' dropping water
on a wet canvas – that is, it will blur. A metaphor takes a step
further than an analogy and insists that one thing is something
else; for example, our computer desktop is a metaphor
because we can leave files on it and put them into folders.

Signifiers and signified

In semiotics, a sign is made up of two elements: the
signifier and the signified. If we took a labelled picture of
a car, the signifier is the word 'car' and the signified is the
image of the car. There is no link between the sound of the
letters used to spell 'car' and the object itself; but if we
called a car a 'brum-brum' there would be an audible link.
This is an important concept because it demonstrates our
capacity to make arbitrary links between the signifier and
the signified.

3.30–3.32 | Signifier and signified
In semiotics, signs are made from two
elements, the signifier (word) and the
signified (image). Usually, there is no
audible link between the sound of the
letters and the image unless the word
is onomatopoeic.

Icon, index and symbol

Building on the use of literal, metaphorical and analogical representations of signs and the distinction between the signifier and the signified, Peirce defined three basic forms of sign: the icon, the index and the symbol.

The *icon* is a literal representation of an image or idea (a line drawing of a car resembles a car).

The *index* indicates meaning (a tyre track represents a car).

The *symbol* is an abstract representation of an image or idea (the written word 'car').

Interestingly, the more visually literate we are, the less reliant on visuals we become. To put this in context, think about the logos we associate with either shoe stores or design studios. There is no hard and fast rule, but those businesses that are associated with less visually literate consumers – such as children's shoes – or that require instant recognition – such as a print design and copy shop – will tend to use icon or index signs for logos, whereas businesses with more sophisticated audiences tend to prefer symbols, usually represented through a discrete use of typography.

Open and closed texts

Roland Barthes, the French literary theorist and philosopher, furthered our understanding of semiotics in the 1960s by establishing the importance of the reader in our interpretation of signs. Barthes' ideas are based on concepts of denotation and connotation. Denotation is the objective reading of an image, for example, 'it is a picture of a red car': connotation is the subjective understanding of that image; that is, the meaning that the reader derives from it based on his or her own learnt conventions and rules (for example, 'the colour and shape remind me of a Ferrari, so it must be fast and sporty...').

Barthes asserted in his best-known essay, *The Death of the Author* (1968), that the reader was in fact the author of a piece of communication, as it was their interpretation that ultimately decided its meaning. Barthes described images without accompanying captions as 'open texts', which meant that they were open to interpretation, and those that were accompanied were 'closed texts' because meaning had been given to the reader.

78

3.38–3.43 | FlashForward

Nissan's FlashForward online promotion, designed by Reactive, uses bold colour, imagery and type to create powerful unambiguous messages (closed texts). The promotion was designed to address the critical 'vehicle consideration' phase of the customer journey, to help establish a lifestyle proposition and to acquaint customers to a broad product range.
The very successful campaign used bold design elements and visual prompts to help guide the user through a series of animated questions.

Preparing images

Images for television

Despite the visual richness and seductive qualities of broadcast television, it is a surprisingly low-resolution medium that needs careful consideration when creating images for its use. Furthermore, the common viewing distance of 10 feet (3 metres) means that images often need to be a little larger than if we were viewing them close-up.

Images and design work for television and other screen-based devices are created at 72 dpi (dots per inch), which compares poorly with print's standard resolution of 300 dpi. Television sets suffer from a low pixel density; despite the relatively large screen size of televisions,

standard definition full-screen images measure only 720x576 pixels (PAL). To put this in perspective, if you were to display a full-screen television image at print resolution 300 dpi it would measure about 2.5 inches by 2 inches (6.5cmx5cm) in size! This is why when you stand very close to a TV set you can see every pixel.

Thankfully, we view our televisions from the comfort of our sofas so we do not notice the pixels. However, it is important to acknowledge that even high-definition television, 1280x720 pixels, is a relatively low-resolution medium, so screen layouts need to be simple and images need to rely on visual impact rather than detail to attract our attention.

3.44–3.63 | *Get Real* short film
Looks can be deceiving… this short film, *Get Real*, was created by Karin Fong and Grant Lau of Imaginary Forces for furniture designer and manufacturer, Herman Miller. It appears to have a more complex composition than it really does. Television uses simpler compositions than print due to lower image resolution; however, they appear more dynamic because they have the ability to move over time, unlike print designs, which remain static.

Images for the Web

While the high-resolution retina display technology featured in the latest Apple products surpasses anything that most consumers have experienced before, web graphics and images are also produced at only 72 dpi. However, images for the Web are noticeably different from television in one vital respect – size.

Web layouts are much more complex than television layouts with apparently small images for both practical and technical reasons. First, the pixel density on a computer monitor, tablet device or smartphone is much higher than on television because their physical screen size is smaller and the screen resolution is much higher. Second, the viewing distance is generally much shorter so images and text can be smaller, allowing the designer more opportunity to increase the number of on-screen elements. Third, larger images take longer to download because their file size is greater. Although file size and download time are less consequential following the advent of broadband, 3G and 4G connections, they are still important factors in countries with less coverage, and for mobile users whose bills are based on data usage.

3.64–3.67 | Udesign Studio website
Designed by Komodo Digital, the UDesign Studio website has beautifully crisp illustrations that are extremely web friendly as the flat areas of colour compress much better than images with much more texture and detail, giving them smaller file sizes that download quicker.

Image format selection

To manage image quality and file sizes effectively for the Web, it is important to choose the right file formats and appropriate image sizes.

There are three common file formats used for still web images: GIF, JPEG and PNG. GIF and PNGs are used for graphic elements, such as logos, where flat colour with crisp edges are important. JPEGs are used for photographs.

As a general principle, images are produced at the exact size required for a web page rather than scaled in the page code. This is to help keep web page size and loading time down to a minimum. The viewing of higher resolution images should be an active choice made by the user; this is why it is a common convention to click on an image to reveal a larger and more detailed version.

Using image libraries

Image libraries supply stock images to designers and license them for specific uses. They are used as a creative alternative to commissioning photographers or illustrators when time and budget are limited. Image libraries used to be physical buildings that you visited in person; or you paid a picture researcher to undertake a search for you. Thanks to the digital age, images are digitized and searchable online although you can still commission researchers to find images on your behalf.

As the media in which designers' work expands, image libraries have also increased the breadth of what they offer. In addition to stock photography and illustration, some image libraries also supply video, animation and even music.

Popular online photo libraries include:

123rf.com

corbisimages.com

gettyimages.com

istockphoto.com

shutterstock.com

How to use them

Image libraries are invaluable tools for designers because they are a source of inspiration both for visual ideas and style of art direction. You can search for concepts as well as topics – for example, 'power' – and refine your searches with additional criteria, such as 'authority AND strength NOT people'.

Image libraries allow designers 'comping' rights, which means that the low-resolution images may be used to mock up designs or provide mood inspiration for a project as long as they are not commercially used or published.

Some image libraries offer free tools for inspiration. For example, the Getty Images 'Moodstream' brainstorming tool lets you set the mood for the project you are researching and creates a full-screen mood film of stirring images, video and music.

Paying for images

Stock images are either rights managed or royalty free. For rights-managed images, the cost of an image will depend on a number of factors: where it will be used, size, distribution, territories, duration of use and the industry it will promote. Purchasing rights-managed images can be very costly, so if several images are required, it is often more cost effective to commission your own photography. Royalty-free images, on the other hand, are relatively inexpensive; you pay a one-off price for the size and quality of the image you want to use.

In the past decade, thanks to the proliferation in digital photography and **Web 2.0** technologies, there has been a marked rise in the number of image libraries offering low-cost images. Many professional and amateur image-makers upload their own images to these sites in return for a percentage of the royalty fees. These sites frequently offer pay-as-you-go credits or subscriptions to access their images.

3.68–3.71 | Library stock
Image libraries also license illustrations and some may provide audio, video and animation, too. The illustrations here were found after conducting a search for 'Interactive Design' on 123RF.

Using image libraries → Industry perspective

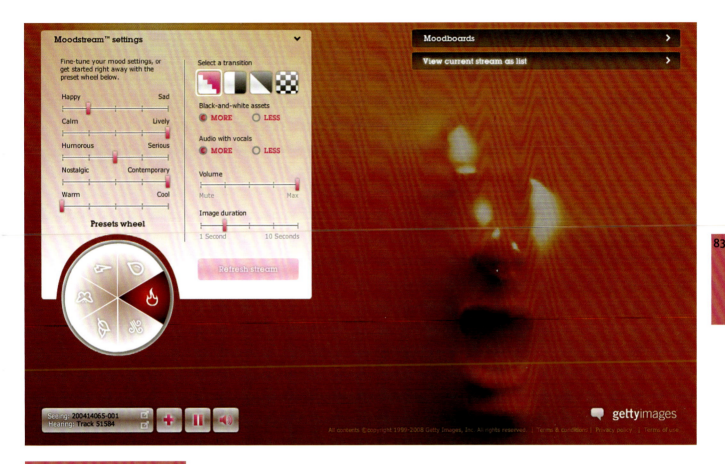

3.72 | The Getty Images Moodstream tool
Content libraries, such as Getty Images, provide an instant source of inspiration for design concepts and art direction. Moodstream is a great ambient tool for brainstorming.

Art direction inspiration

If you're just looking for stylistic inspiration, why not look through online sourcebooks and agents' websites for designers, image-makers, illustrators and photographers? Here are a few:

agencyrush.com

behance.net

contact-creative.com

eyemade.com

handsomefrank.com

horton-stephens.com

magnumphotos.com

Industry perspective:
Tim Beard, Bibliothèque

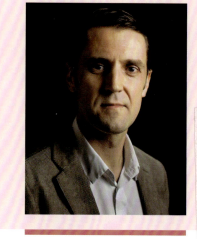

Client
Multinet

Brief
Brand creation including strategy, naming and visual identity for a new telecoms brand that provides high-speed Internet access to emerging markets.

Agency
Bibliothèque

Solution
A single line of communication, connecting communities where online demand sits alongside limited infrastructure. The logo is the first to exploit the new multi-touch hardware of smartphones and tablets.

Interview with Tim Beard, Founding Partner of Bibliothèque
Bibliothèque is an independent design studio based in London, founded in 2003 by Tim Beard, Jonathon Jeffrey and Mason Wells. It has earned an international reputation as an innovative company working in the fields of brand identity, spatial and digital design.

3.74–3.75 | Ollo interactive logo
To help create an emotional connection between Ollo and its new audience, Bibliothèque have designed an interactive logo that reflects its engaging and playful brand values.

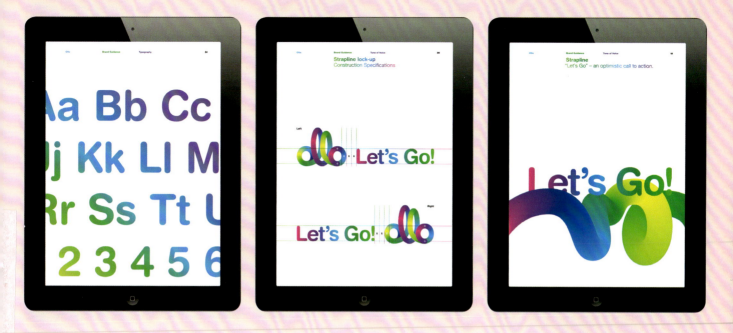

3.76–3.78 | Applying an identity system
Ollo brand guidelines show how the identity system should be applied across a range of touchpoints.

It is a challenging brief – were the requirements clear from the outset? Or did you develop the brief in partnership with your client?
Briefs are usually slightly fluid. Generally, a client comes to us with a project in mind, and it's our job to drill down beneath the surface, to ensure that the project we are going to deliver will fulfil their requirements. The brief from Multinet was relatively short, but you could see that they had great ambition for the project, and they had a clear aim to create something that felt very different in the marketplace.

What research did you undertake prior to starting your design work?
Part of our design process is always an immersion, research and analysis phase. This lets us really get to grips with the client and the market they are working in, and to develop a full understanding of all the touchpoints. A big chunk of this phase will be a detailed examination of the competitive landscape, which for Ollo was an overview of many of the world's biggest telecoms companies, and their brand personalities. It can also really help clarify the brand ambition of what they want to be or, more importantly, what they don't want to be.

What were the main findings from your research?
I think that the most important out-take from the research was the incredibly rigid nature of most of the brands and their identities. We were very keen from the outset that Ollo would be engaging and fun, rather than corporate and inflexible. We wanted people to be able to engage with the logo, and play with it, and creating a stronger and more emotional brand connection – rather than just letting the identity sit as a fixed lock up, in the corner of a page, never to be touched. So brand expression, with the logo as the core driver, seemed like an exciting place to aim.

How did you arrive at the name Ollo?
The naming process was also a very big stage in the early part of the project. We investigated thousands of possible names. Creating a brand name that is able to be registered in all the countries and in all of the sectors required is an extremely difficult undertaking these days. And thus, new brand names are becoming stranger and stranger – or evolving into combinations of several words, creating new words. We wanted the brand name to be more of a sound than a specific word, something that wouldn't stand or fall on its translation into local languages. 'Ollo' was the middle of the word 'follow', which had a good social networking connotation. Also, it was the name that offered up the most, in terms of its creative execution. And that's always a very important consideration for us.

Industry perspective:
Tim Beard, Bibliothèque

How does the logotype reflect your brand strategy?

'The single line of communication, connecting people in areas of limited infrastructure' was the explanation of the brand story. And this single line obviously translated well into the looping and colourful form that became the Ollo logo. The 'fun' aspect, reflecting a strategic aim to engage a younger audience, really came to life with its touch-responsive iteration.

Your logotype is literally interactive. Was this envisaged early on in your design development?

As the logo concept started to become refined, we quickly realized that making it engaging in some way, beyond a fixed form, was going to be much more exciting for everyone involved. So as it was being developed, and ahead of our first big creative presentation, we got in touch with programmers at FIELD, and we explained that we felt it could come to life as a single, but elastic line – always returning to the form of the logo. And they helped breathe life into it.

Is there an inherent danger in undermining an identity if you let the user play with it?

Possibly, yes. But I think that the strength in emotional connection that would be created outweighs the dangers of letting the end user play with it. And also, the logo itself was always designed to snap back to its original state, so the form of the logo was always returned to.

Why did you build a software tool to create visual language?

We appointed FIELD, who developed a piece of software that would allow us to refine the elasticity, the thickness of the line and all its dynamic properties. It was an amazing piece of science. We then used this to decide on the final properties of the logo and its movement. It was the only way to enable us to create the range of expression and dynamic properties required. A fixed set of 'expressive' logo lock ups would simply not have done the job, or told the story.

Could you explain your choice of colour used for the Ollo brand?

We didn't want to provide a fixed and 'corporate' colour for Ollo. To us, it was much more fun and reflective of the brand personality to create a form that embodied all colour. The gradient of colour along the line was then used in other brand and marketing pieces. It also felt a little bit different to the large number of brands who establish themselves with a fixed colour of a specific tone of red, blue or orange, etc. A rainbow of colour seemed more reflective of the 'global marketplace' that Ollo was directed at.

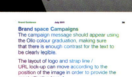

Were there any particular challenges that you had to overcome in developing the brand?

I guess our main challenge was the creation of something truly unique. We are always our own harshest critics, and producing something that feels good enough to push out into the world is always a major challenge for us.

When you push the boundaries in any design discipline, you can run into challenges at a board level that can derail the process. However, our experience with the board team at Multinet was great. They were enthusiastic and energized with our response to the brief, and keen to make the project something very special.

And to deliver a great project, you usually need a great brief and a great client. This one had both.

3.79–3.84 | Identity system continued
Ollo brand guidelines show how the identity system should be applied across a range of touchpoints.

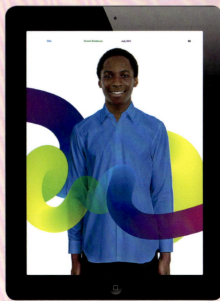

Workshop III:
Taste after taste

The following workshop is intended to help you explore your visual associations and sensibilities when making colour choices. The workshop is planned to last two hours and can be undertaken as a solo activity, although created artefacts would benefit from group discussion at the end.

Background

As humans, we have a multitude of senses and Aristotle (384BC–322BC) is credited with the classification of our five traditional senses of sight, sound, smell, taste and touch. However, our sense of taste, which also has five recognized categories – sweetness, bitterness, sourness, saltiness and umami – has only relatively recently been agreed upon. The last category, 'umami' or savouriness, was only recognized as a scientific term in 1985.

Brief

The object of this workshop is to visually explore our sense of taste by trying to represent these five taste categories using images and colour. Our findings are going to be collated in a mosaic that depicts our notions of taste. The workshop can be divided into two halves. Steps 1–6 involve the visual association of colour and image, whereas Step 7 is about the practical application of selecting a set of connected web colours.

Note: You may choose to use this exercise as an opportunity to become more familiar with online image libraries by finding and selecting **comping images** to use.

  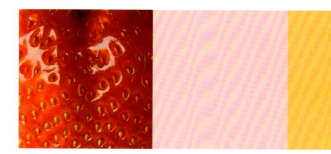

3.85 | Depicting a term
The row of images and colour collected by Luke Emmerson is an example of how the term 'sweet' could be depicted by using literal, metaphorical and abstract images, as well as natural and cultural associations.

BODY **LINK** *HOVER* **ACTIVE** VISITED

Step 1 – Create a grid
In a graphics package of your choice (for example, Adobe Photoshop), create a document that is 500x500 pixels, then divide the image into 100x100 pixels using guides to create a 5x5 pixels square grid.

Step 2 – Literal image
Think of images that literally represent each of the five categories of taste: sweet, bitter, sour, salty and savoury. Find representative images and place them in the first column grid. 'Literal' is defined as understanding words in their usual or most basic form without metaphor or exaggeration.

Step 3 – Metaphorical image
Next, find images that metaphorically represent each of the categories and place them next to their literal counterparts in the adjacent column. A metaphor is a thing that is perceived to represent or symbolize something else: for example, a chrysalis is a metaphor for change or a light bulb is a metaphor for an idea.

Step 4 – Abstract image
Find images that abstractly represent each taste category and place them in the third column. 'Abstract', for the purpose of this exercise, is defined as a non-literal idea attempting to represent reality through shape or texture; for example, a motion-blurred shape is often used to represent speed.

Step 5 – Natural colour
Choose a single colour for each category of taste. The colours must have a natural association with the sense. For example, we might associate fire with the colour red. Fill each square of the fourth column with carefully considered shades of your chosen colours.

Step 6 – Cultural colour
Similar to step 5, choose colours that represent each category with a cultural connotation; for example, we often associate purple with luxury or royalty. Again, fill each square with your chosen colour in the fifth column.

Step 7 – Web colours
Now that you have explored the categories through image and colour, it is time for a more practical application. Imagine what body text colour you would choose to represent each taste category on a web page, and the four should link state colours too: link, hover, active and visited.

Either extend your current document by 500 pixels or create a new document that is 500x500 pixels divided by another 5x5 grid. The background colour should be white; and for each of the five categories write the words body, link, hover, active and visited in adjacent boxes. Each word should be written in a representative colour of your choice.

Although it may seem appropriate to have the body text in pure black, you may decide to have something a little lighter with a hue to represent each taste category. Also, think carefully about the link state colours – how should an active link appear when clicked? How should a link look once visited?

The mosaic is now complete
Share your mosaic with others and discuss whether they have similar or different visual associations with notions of taste.

3.86 | Representation
This row shows web colours that could represent the term 'power'. Text size text and background colour often affects our choice of text colour.

In the last 150 years, we have witnessed many wonderful innovations in the fields of communication and narrative storytelling – from Alexander Graham Bell's telephone and David Edward Hughes's wireless telegraphy to John Logie Baird's television and beyond; but none of them have replaced or endured as long the Phoenician's 3,000-year-old idea to replace pictograms with a simple set of symbols to represent sounds – namely letters.

Digital typography

Letters form words that make up languages, that in turn signify ideas, actions and thoughts. Letters have built the bedrock on which civilizations have communicated and shared their beliefs, history, knowledge, laws and literature with their peoples and their descendants for thousands of years.

Johannes Gutenberg's movable type technology and his printed 42-line Bible in the fifteenth century transformed the way we communicate through greater access to the published word. Similarly, Sir Tim Berners-Lee's World Wide Web in the late-twentieth century has revolutionized our ability to access, share and communicate the digital word.

With this long history of letters and their communication, it is unsurprising that a great deal of human endeavour has gone into the development of letterforms, and the syntax or rules that govern the organization of words. Typography, which is the art of arranging letterforms, is both the practical and visual expression of written language. Typography is not just a humble carrier of words to aid linguistic meaning. It can convey semantic meaning, too, because typography in size, shape, colour, placement and movement can express important messages of its own.

The following sections will help you to understand the fundamental characteristics of typography, its conventions and application in a variety of digital contexts and visual forms. In the process, you will begin to recognize how important great typography is to both the practical realization and creative expression of your work.

4

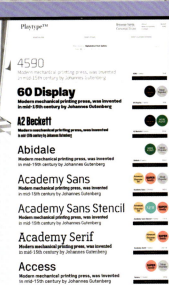

4.01–4.04 | Playtype foundry
Playtype is a typographic foundry set up by Danish design agency e-Types. It bridges the virtual/physical divide with an online type foundry and a concept store in Copenhagen.

Top: Concept store interior.

Above right: Store Playtype.

Above left: About Playtype landing page.

Bottom: Browse fonts landing page.

Fundamentals

To understand and appreciate the application of typography, it is essential to first become familiar with the basic characteristics and features of letterforms. Through their understanding, you can diagnose issues with a particular typeface and communicate what characteristics you are looking for when discussing typeface selection with fellow designers.

Two important terms to begin with are 'typeface' and 'font'. These common terms are not strictly interchangeable and have different meanings. A typeface is a set of one or more fonts that share a stylistic unity and form part of a type family. A font is a single character set of a particular typeface and size. Letters, numbers and other symbols that make up a character set are individually known as 'glyphs'.

Measuring type

Type size is traditionally measured in points (pt), with 72 points equivalent to an inch (2.54 cm). For screen-based design, type is increasingly measured in pixels (px) and in 'ems'. Although a point is a fixed measurement, two fonts can appear to be of different proportions when they share the same point size. This is due to differences in fonts' relative 'x' heights and widths.

Type size is measured from the lowest descender of a font's letterforms to just above the highest ascender, and a font's x-height is measured from its baseline to the height of the lowercase x. Therefore, those fonts with short ascenders and descenders, or tall x-heights, will appear relatively larger than others. Similarly, fonts with less height variation between its upper-case and lower-case letters will also appear larger.

The width of letterforms will also affect a font's relative size. A font's point size relates to its height only and not its width, so condensed fonts will visually appear smaller than those with broader widths. The width of a font is normally expressed in characters per pica and this measurement is used to estimate how much text will fit into an allotted space.

4.05 | An anatomy of type
This diagram identifies common terminology used when describing letterforms.

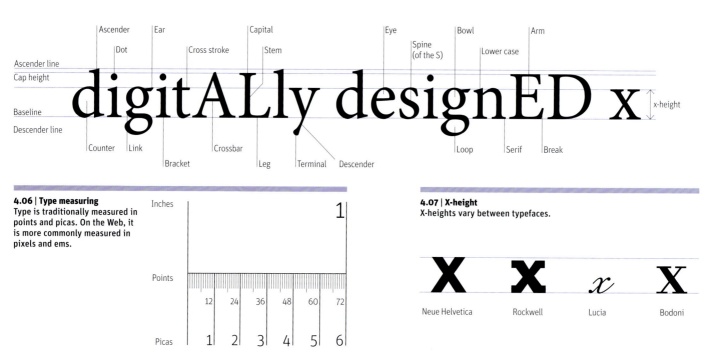

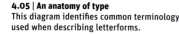

4.06 | Type measuring
Type is traditionally measured in points and picas. On the Web, it is more commonly measured in pixels and ems.

4.07 | X-height
X-heights vary between typefaces.

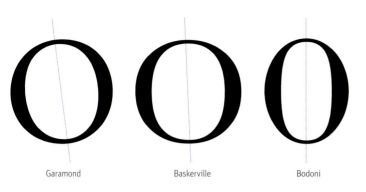

Garamond   Baskerville   Bodoni

Kerning

LOVE
TYPE

Leading

Tracking

93

Stress

The stress refers to the angle of the thin stroke in rounded letterforms. Historically, 'old style' serif typefaces, such as Caslon, have inclined or 'oblique' stresses whereas 'modern' serifs, such as Bodoni, have vertical. Typefaces of the 'transitional' period have semi-oblique stresses, for example, Baskerville.

Ligatures

A ligature is the joining of two or more characters to create a single glyph. Ligatures have their origins in ancient manuscripts and were designed to stop letter shapes colliding. The most prominent ligature is the joining of 'f' and 'i' to make 'fi'.

Letter spacing – tracking and kerning

Letter spacing is measured in ems. An em is a relative measurement and is traditionally based on the width of the widest capital letter of an alphabet, namely the letter 'M'. General letter spacing is known as 'tracking' whereas individual spacing between two letters is called 'kerning'. Note: an em is now commonly used to describe the relative height of letterforms too, where 1 em = the point size of the font.

Leading

The spacing between lines of type is known as 'leading'. This historical term comes from the days of moveable metal type when different thicknesses of lead were placed between lines of type to aid readability. Leading is expressed in points, too. For example, 10/12pt is 10pt type on 12pt leading.

Classification and selection

The digital age has heralded an explosion in choice and availability of typefaces. Almost all typefaces are available in downloadable digital form from type foundry websites. Type creation and manipulation software has encouraged a whole generation of typographers to create their own fonts for individual clients or for general sale and online distribution. Searching The Web, it is easy to find free fonts that are either very expressive or look very similar to classic typefaces that are renowned for their practical qualities. However, not all of them possess the same attention to detail and versatility.

Understanding how typefaces are classified, as well as their individual features, qualities and history will help you to make informed selection choices. This section will explain the very basics of type classification and selection. Suggestions for further reading are available in the bibliography.

Styles and weights

Versatile typefaces come in a series of styles known as 'weights'. For example, the Neue Helvetica typeface family shows not only the standard regular, bold and italic, but also a whole range of different stroke weights.

In the past 25 years, we have also seen the growth of 'super families', which include Serif, Sans Serif and Slab Serif versions of popular typefaces such as Museo, Stone, Officina and Thesis. These super families are designed to work harmoniously together and give a visual consistency to a design across a variety of uses.

4.11 | Choice of typeface
Apps like FontBook 2.0 make it simpler to view and make informed typeface choices.

4.12–4.13 | Neue Helvetica
Linotype's Neue Helvetica family (1983) is based on Max Miedinger's 1957 original Helvetica.

Categories

Typefaces have a rich history and their stylistic development has evolved over hundreds of years in response to advances in technology, aesthetics, commerce and our growing understanding of legibility and readability. For designers, selecting typefaces is not simply an arbitrary choice; it requires both an appreciation of the practical value of a typeface and an understanding of its inherent historical associations.

Aa Serif

Roman inscriptions inspired serif typefaces. The term 'serif' describes the angular details at the ends of letter strokes. Old-style serifs date back to the fifteenth century and serifs today are associated with traditional book and newspaper publishing.

Aa Sans Serif

Sans Serifs or 'Grotesks' came into prominence at the end of the eighteenth century, partly as an aesthetic reaction to the over ornamentation of serifs and, more practically, as a need for typefaces with greater legibility. Sans Serifs are commonly used for signage and information graphics, and work well on screen.

Aa Slab Serif

Slab Serifs are characterized by thick block-like serifs. They first came into use at the beginning of the nineteenth century, and are used for headlines because of their bold authoritative nature. For this reason, heavy slab serifs are used sparingly as they are uncomfortable to read for more than a few lines of continuous reading.

Aa Script

Script typefaces replicate handwritten or hand-rendered lettering and visually express the personality of the writer or era with which the style of lettering is associated. Script typefaces can be subdivided into Calligraphic, Casual, Formal and Handwritten amongst others.

Aa Display

Display typefaces provide the designer with a powerful visual language, where creative expression is prioritized over legibility. They were first used on posters in the nineteenth century to create impact for advertising and have been used to convey promotional messages ever since.

Aa Blackletter

Blackletter typefaces are based on German manuscripts dating back to the twelfth century and were widely used throughout Europe before the eighteenth century. Blackletter typefaces are historically associated with Johannes Gutenberg who used this style for his printed 42-line Bible.

✠ ⤷ ✪ ❀ Symbol

Symbols consist of decorative elements, icons and other glyphs rather than regular Latin characters and numbers. They are used to embellish or decorate written text – for example, Victorian wood ornaments – or provide an alternative symbolic language for information graphics – for example, a series of representative sports icons.

丙丞丢串 Non-Western

Non-Western or non-Latin is a group term used to describe typefaces that are not based on Roman letterforms. Typefaces that use Middle Eastern Sanskrit or Chinese, Japanese and Korean character sets fall into this category.

Find

FontBook™ home page

Classes

Subclasses

Subclass range

FontBook 2011

FontBook 2006

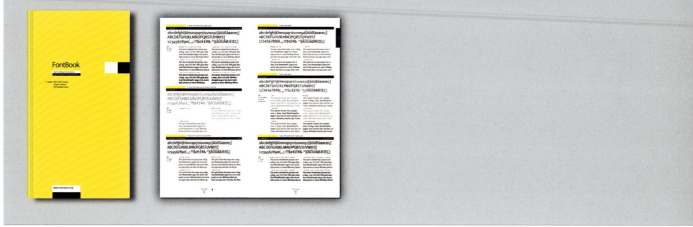

4.14 | FontBook 2.0

This awarding-winning app is a comprehensive typographic reference tool containing the libraries of over 130 international type foundries, and covers nearly 37,000 typefaces from 8,000+ font families. The extensive content can be intuitively browsed, searched, layered, moved, scrolled and combined like a collection of maps. In comparison to its printed predecessor, it makes searching for typeface a quicker, simpler and more informative user experience. It is also easier to update, cheaper to produce and more environmentally friendly, too.

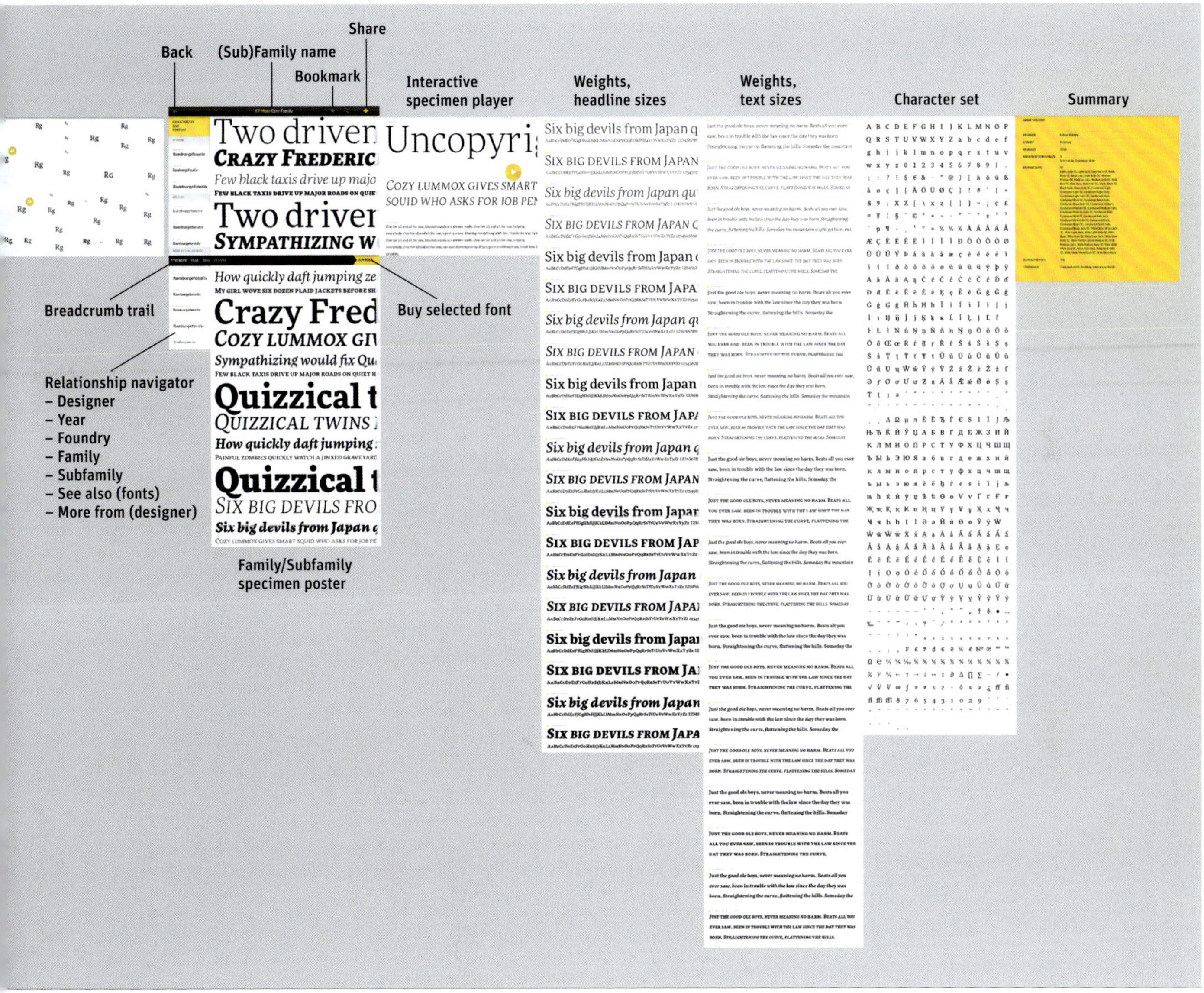

Back

(Sub)Family name

Share

Bookmark

Interactive
specimen player

Weights,
headline sizes

Weights,
text sizes

Character set

Summary

Breadcrumb trail

Buy selected font

Relationship navigator
– Designer
– Year
– Foundry
– Family
– Subfamily
– See also (fonts)
– More from (designer)

Family/Subfamily
specimen poster

Legibility and readability

There are many rules and conventions regarding the legibility and readability of type for both print publishing and screen-based design. General principles will be covered here in this chapter, along with more specific advice given on television graphics, web publishing and design for small devices.

Typeface selection

Both serif and sans serifs are great for continuous reading, although the context and a typeface's individual characteristics will be decisive factors in making your selection.

Serif letterforms are distinctive and their relatively low x-heights make reading easy. However, for the smallest legible type sizes, sans serifs are better because of their more even stroke weight and taller x-heights, making them clearer to see. For this reason, sans serifs are particularly good for television graphics where legibility at small sizes is paramount.

Avoid long passages with bold or capitalized type as they become difficult and uncomfortable to read due to the similarity of letterform shapes.

Leading

The amount of leading required will depend on the x-height of the font used and the line length. The larger the x-height or the longer the line, the more leading will be required to help the reader differentiate between lines.

Tracking

Relatively few typefaces have been designed with screen use in mind. Verdana, by type designer Matthew Carter, was designed for screen use and benefits from loose letter spacing to increase on-screen legibility.

Line length

Ideal line length is a topical readability issue with the advent of high-resolution screens and people's acceptance of blogs, which have increased average reading line lengths. The generally accepted optimum is 60–75 characters per line (cpl); any longer and people start to lose their place. However, recent studies have shown that line lengths of 95 cpl line speeds up reading (Shaikh, 2005) and many popular blogs often have line lengths of 100 cpl.

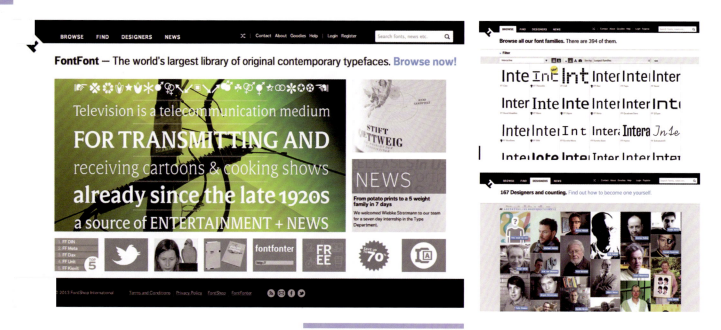

4.15–4.17 | FontFont website
Edenspiekermann's redesign of Fontfont's website makes type identification and selection a pleasurable online experience.

Alignment

Left aligned text with a ragged right edge is commonly used for reading continuous passages. This alignment ensures that word spacing is consistent and aids readability. Ranged-left text columns are widely used for on-screen use.

Centre aligned implies text centred in the middle of each line. It creates a pleasing visual symmetry; however, it is unsuitable for continuous reading due to the variable starting position of each line.

Right aligned is rarely used as the reader has to work hard to find the beginning of each line and this should be strictly avoided for passages of continuous reading.

Justified text introduces variations in word spacing to match line lengths. It creates a pleasing visual symmetry to columns of text at the potential expense of readability. If type size and leading are too great for the column width, 'rivers' of space will appear and reduce readability.

Hyphenation can be used to make more even line lengths, but care is needed to avoid too much hyphenation, which would reduce readability.

Widows and orphans are single words and short lines at the end of a paragraph (an orphan) or at the start/end of a new column (a widow), and should also be avoided where possible. This is difficult to achieve on The Web when the designer has less control over the final formatting of copy, and the user has some control over the text displayed in the browser.

4.18 | Readability
The following diagram illustrates many of the constituent factors for increasing readibility.

Leading

The amount of leading required will depend on the x-height of the font used and line length. The larger the x-height or the longer the line, the more leading will be required to help the reader differentiate between lines. This paragraph is set in Minion Pro Regular 7pt on 9pt leading.

The amount of leading required will depend on the x-height of the font used and line length. The larger the x-height or the longer the line, the more leading will be required to help the reader differentiate between lines. This paragraph is set in Verdana Regular 7pt on 10pt leading.

The amount of leading required will depend on the x-height of the font used and line length. The larger the x-height or the longer the line, the more leading will be required to help the reader differentiate between lines. This paragraph is set in Verdana Regular 7pt on 14pt leading.

Tracking

Tracking affects text readability; this line of text has tracking set at -50/1000ems.
Tracking affects text readability; this line of text has tracking set at 0/1000ems.
Tracking affects text readability; this line of text has tracking set at 100/1000ems.

Line length

This line of text is the ideal line length as it contains 60–75 characters.
This line contains about 95 characters, which a study suggests is the optimum for speed reading.
This line of text contains over 100 characters, which is the line length used by many popular blogs.

Alignment

Left aligned text with a ragged right edge is commonly used for reading continuous passages. This alignment ensures that word spacing is consistent and aids readability. Ranged-left text columns are widely used for on-screen use.

Centre aligned implies text centred in the middle of each line. It creates a pleasing visual symmetry; however, it is unsuitable for continuous reading due to the variable starting position of each line.

Right aligned is rarely used as the reader has to work hard to find the beginning of each line and this should be strictly avoided for passages of continuous reading.

Justified text introduces variations in word spacing to match line lengths. It creates a pleasing visual symmetry to columns of text at the potential expense of readability. If type size and leading are too great for the column width, rivers of space will appear and reduce readability.

Using type on television

Type plays a different part on television to its usual role online or in print. Audio and video are the preferred media for driving narrative and delivering programme content, with text left to perform subordinate functions such as programme titling, captions, subtitles and news information graphics.

Apart from media preference, there are technical reasons that limit the application and style of on-screen typography. As mentioned in the previous chapter (p.80), one limiting factor is television's relatively poor image resolution in comparison to print. Standard definition television is only 720x576 pixels (PAL) so when the image is stretched over a 40-inch (100-cm) television screen, you need a viewing distance of about 10 feet (3 metres) just so you do not notice the individual pixels!

Screen resolution and users' established viewing preference for watching television from the comfort of their sofas means that body text should be no smaller than 24 pixels high. This large type size, together with eye fatigue associated with reading from a back-illuminated screen, makes television a problematic device for the continuous reading of text.

When type is used to display information or subtitles, sans serifs are often preferred to serifs for legibility, as the thin strokes of serifs tend to disappear at small sizes.

To reduce eye strain, light text is often displayed over darker backgrounds to reduce illumination. However strong contrasts in hue or luminance should be avoided to stop unwanted glow and distortion occurring around objects: this is called 'blooming'.

4.19–4.22 | Idents
BBC2 channel idents use typography as the main visual device for communicating seasonal or themed programming.

4.23–4.31 | Use of typographic textures
TFO's *Les Bleus de Ramville* title sequence, by Oily Film Company Inc, uses typographic textures to evoke nostalgia for a senior hockey team based in the fictional Canadian town of Ramville.

Using type as image

After the primary visual shapes of circles, squares and triangles, letters and numbers are the forms we most readily recognize. Unsurprisingly, this familiarity with the shape of type has often led designers to use them as an expressive form.

Type as image can be playful and engaging, and is often used to reinforce brand values. The animated channel idents for BBC2 in the United Kingdom are a long-running example. Typographic elements can also be used as texture to create a nostalgic atmosphere as seen in the television title sequence for the French Canadian drama *Les Bleus de Ramville*.

Type is also used at scale to create architectural or sculptural qualities that convey notions of importance and authority. The BBC's title sequence for *How We Built Britain* employs these virtues. At other times, typography can be heavily abstracted or concealed to confuse or provide intrigue; these intentions were present in Julius Popp's Bit.code installation in the Decode exhibition at the V&A Museum in London in 2009–10.

The only limit to type as an expressive medium is that it remains tied to its linguistic origins. In an increasingly globalized world, there is an underlying requirement for images that tell stories without words or need for translation. Therefore, typographic images that rely on the viewer to understand their implicit linguistic and cultural meaning may defy translation and so creative intention will be lost.

4.32–4.38 | Using the sculptural qualities of type
BBC's *How We Built Britain* title sequence uses the sculptural qualities of type to create a sense of importance.

4.39–4.40 | Typographic abstraction
Julius Popp's Bit.code installation was part of the Decode exhibition at the V&A Museum in London in 2009–10.

Using type for information

Typography has a long history in helping convey complex messages and information. Its ability to communicate simple instructions or sophisticated data with impartial authority or passionate appeal is testament to the versatility of typography and the skill of the designer.

Data is a bountiful resource in the digital age; using it to visualize trends, tell stories or illustrate issues has become a huge growth area for design in recent years, with kinetic typography and animated information graphics proving popular mediums for this.

Information design through data visualization does not just tell the stories of past events or deliver impersonal facts; it has the ability to visualize ongoing issues for us to share or present personalized factual information to lay bare certain truths.

Playspent.org exploits the immersive and shareable nature of social games to raise awareness of what it is like to live on the breadline. The games use a combination of authoritative serifs and impersonal condensed sans serif typefaces to guide the user through a series of stark choices with bleak outcomes.

In a similar financial vein, You vs John Paulson is an online information graphic that uses your annual salary, comparative statistics and real-time updates to illustrate how much the renowned financial trader earns in comparison to you.

Finally, data can be used to automatically generate images that illustrate issues. Onformative, a Berlin-based design studio specializing in generative design, used virtual plant growth to visualize the air quality of various cities. Organic letterforms of each city's name were used to make the visual connection between the city and its air quality.

4.41–4.42 | *Playspent.org*
Public awareness and fundraising online campaign developed by the agency, McKinney.

YOU
vs.
JOHN PAULSON

How long does it take super-trader John Paulson to earn your annual income?

$ 100,000

10.0 minutes.

John Paulson makes your annual income

t f Share.

How Much?

Dirty	Stinking	Rotten
4.9 b.	**13** m.	**49,000** yrs.
In 2009 John Paulson earned $4.9 billion.	On average, over $13 million a day.	Years would it take you to earn the same.

0 Min. 46 Sec.

In the time you've been here, John would have made...

$7,231

0:46

Know many people who make $555,900 an hour?

t f Share.

Things you could buy with $4.9b

Manchester United F.C, The New York Yankees and the Dallas Cowboys. Combined.

x4,900 Nights with Demi Moore*

The South Pacific nation of Fiji

Relatively speaking:

John dropping $400k is the equivalent of you buying a giant pretzel.

Perhaps it's time to start trading?
Mahi online forex trading launches in 2012

E-mail me an invitation

● **MahiFX**

Who is John Paulson?

"How long does it take John Paulson to earn your annual income?"

t f Tell your friends.

105

4.44–4.46 | Generative typography
Onformative's 'Growing Data' project is a generative design visualization of cities' air pollution levels.

4.43 | You vs John Paulson
Real-time information graphic by *mahifx.com*, which makes interesting salary comparisons between you and stock market trader John Paulson.

Type on the Web

The World Wide Web has transformed the way we access, read, write, interact and publish text. While web content has enjoyed 20 years of fast-paced evolution, it is only in the last couple of years that web designers have been given the typographic control they have always craved.

The freedom with which we can browse information from established publishers, read independent blogs or create our own blogs is truly revolutionary. Copy is written concisely in byte sizes to enable scan reading, with phrases carefully chosen to appear high in search results, and text-based hypertext links used to navigate content. Web designers today can focus on designing dynamic templates for web editorial that attract users and maximize their ability to browse content quickly.

Designing templates rather than final content is one difference between designing a website and a printed magazine. However, until the introduction of **web fonts** in 2009, another key difference was lack of typographic choice and control. Until this moment, typeface selection for text content was limited to the web-safe system fonts available on the end user's computer. Web fonts are stored remotely on the server and are temporarily downloaded to display web pages. This freedom to make more considered font choices, combined with the layout control of Cascading Style Sheets (CSS), has finally given the designer full command over typographic styling.

While web fonts have given designers much greater choice of typefaces, this freedom does come with a number of important additional considerations. Not all web fonts are well defined or as suitable for on-screen reading as web-safe fonts such as Arial, Georgia and Verdana. Typefaces like Verdana use 'text hinting' to improve legibility at small sizes. Text hinting is additional data or instructions on how to display the outline of a typeface at particular font sizes. Well-hinted typefaces have detailed instructions on how to display fonts at numerous font sizes and weights.

In addition to font hinting, designers need to be careful to choose web fonts that have extensive character sets that include glyphs for all central European characters to ensure readability of text in multiple languages. Similar care needs to be taken when selecting web fonts for languages that use non-Latin letterforms and characters.

Type on the Web → Using type on small and dedicated devices

e-Types created a new visual identity
for Denmark's famous Jazzhouse, which
included the design of a custom-made
typeface and website. The latter makes
full use of web fonts and the designer's
mastery over typographic detail.

Using type on small and dedicated devices

These days, the digital world on smartphones and tablets is beautifully crisp with screen resolutions well in excess of 150 pixels per inch (ppi), making individual pixels virtually undetectable to the human eye. For typography, this means beautifully rendered type that is as clear and legible as in print. So are there any typographic considerations that we need to note when designing for the small screen?

4.53–4.58 | Revamped user interface design
Jason Bishop's user-interface design for the revamped 2011 Sony Reader and the global Reader Store. The reader has a resolution of 600x800 pixels with a minimum readable font size of 6pt. The design required extensive testing from engineers in Tokyo and San Jose to get the responsiveness of the touch screen and the refresh of the E Ink display just right. Monochromatic interfaces are a particular challenge for design as colour is often used to create order and give a perceived focus to the user.

The simple answer is yes.

Although smartphones have high-resolution screens, they are physically many times smaller than laptops or desktop monitors. Therefore, web pages that are not adapted for mobile viewing will appear too small and deliver an uncomfortable reading experience. Many websites resolve this by creating separate Cascading Style Sheets (CSS) for mobile devices, which reformat web pages for optimal viewing.

While high-resolution screens have reduced legibility issues attached to screen reading, bright liquid crystal display (LCD) screens will cause eye fatigue with sustained reading use. However, many eBook readers use E Ink technology, which have matt screens that are not back illuminated, giving a very similar reading experience to paper. Amazon's Kindle, which incorporates E Ink, also uses proprietary fonts specifically designed to increase readability.

Despite the issue with sustained reading time for LCD screens, they have a distinct legibility advantage over previous CRT (Cathode Ray Tube) technology. LCD screens use sub-pixel rendering to increase the apparent resolution of the screen. Each pixel is composed of three individual red, green and blue sub-pixels that can be used to anti-alias text with greater detail. While these individual colour components are not visible to the human eye, by manipulating them at a sub-pixel level, both images and type appear perceptibly sharper.

Whether users make a choice between the attraction and convenience of colour LCD displays over the comfort and readability of E Ink, only time will tell...

4.59–4.60 | Kindle's use of technologies
Amazon's Kindle Paperwhite uses E Ink technology for a better reading experience. The Kindle Fire uses LCD technology like many other colour tablet devices, which is great for viewing images and video, but works less well for sustained reading use.

Industry perspective:
Mathias Jespersen, e-Types

Agency

e-Types, Copenhagen, Denmark

Interview with Mathias Jespersen, Senior Digital Consultant

Mathias has worked at e-Types for 12 years, first as a designer and more latterly as a Senior Digital Consultant where he has been helping transform e-Types' considerable brand strategy and typographic expertise into beautifully crafted digital solutions for clients.

4.61 | Mathias Jespersen

4.62–4.63 | e-Types' online type foundry
Playtype, e-Types' online type foundry, was a breakthrough website for the agency as it showcased their online typographic credentials.

e-Types is an unusual agency because you appear to design everything from a client's brand strategy to custom-made typefaces and their website. Is this why clients come to you?

Our clients are beginning to realize that we can provide this now. We definitely want to offer this full service. Of course, we're not the 'database guys' or Google search specialists, but given the fact that we develop their brand strategy and visual identity, we can really see the benefit for our clients in designing their web presence as it's such an important part of the way they communicate.

How long does it take you to develop your visual identity projects, which include new typefaces?

It varies a lot. Some new fonts are reworks of previously designed fonts so it's fast paced. Then on the other hand, we might work on a typeface for a newspaper where Jonas and Jens may create 28 weights of a font family that might take forever! It varies so much.

110

What makes a good web font?

Good question. A couple of years ago I would have said legibility, but that's not so important now with retina displays and web browsers are becoming much more efficient at rendering stuff. I would say identity in its expressiveness and clarity. It is refreshing not to have to see Arial, Times and Verdana all of the time.

How do these considerations affect the design of a new typeface?

I think they don't, to be short. The purpose of the font is the most relevant consideration. On the *Hitman* project, we wanted to create this virtual secret space that was a communication forum between the hitman and a clandestine organization. Therefore, we created a font to make it feel atmospheric in a low-fi 80s kind of way. Obviously, if there are technical considerations, such as if it has to work on television, we know it has to have a certain x-height, but that's just detail.

What software tools do you use to create typefaces?

We use FontLab and then we use various tools for testing how they look in the browser. The biggest challenge for our fonts when optimizing them for The Web is 'hinting' because of the ways in which different operating systems interpret them.

Do you work with a regular grid system when designing web pages?

We tend to create our own. It gives us the freedom to reflect some of the ideas created for the offline solutions. A lot of designers are really happy with the 960 or 1140 grid systems, which are really good for a base. However, we tend to design and code our own.

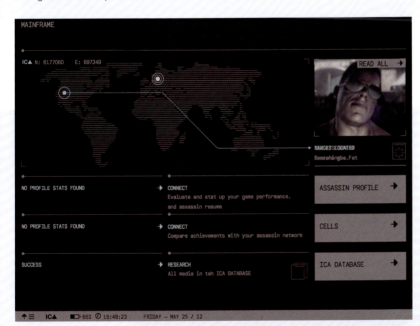

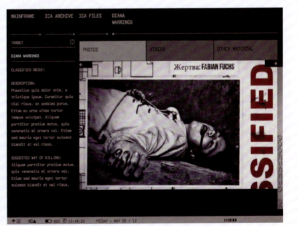

4.64–4.66 | *Hitman*
This app for IO Interactive's *Hitman* uses a custom-made retro typeface to give the game a lo-fi 1980s computer game look and feel.

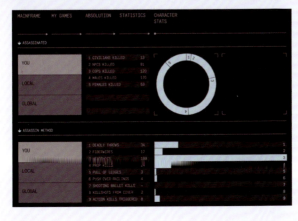

Industry perspective:
Mathias Jespersen, e-Types

Your web design for Gottlieb Paludan Architects uses an unusual floating navigation bar – why did you decide to use this?

We wanted to do something different. Most architects have a full-screen image with small text, but our client wanted a more editorial approach so we came up with a magazine front page with the stories they want to tell highlighted in different boxes. We just thought it would make sense for the content to be in focus all of the time and rather than have a menu bar at the top, we decided to give it an app look by having a navigation bar at the bottom of the screen.

Your webpage layouts have a lot of typographic attention to detail, for example, 'illuminated letters' at the beginning of new articles. Does this create challenges when your clients edit and manage content?

Yes it does! Over the years, we have had some really well thought out projects – well designed and well implemented – that sadly did not work perfectly in reality once the client took over the handling of the design. However, we can only blame ourselves because we hadn't been clear from the start that we were producing an advanced design for them, so they needed to take the time to create content and find the right images. In the last couple of years, this is the first thing we have emphasized to the client. Content strategy is such an important part of successful web design.

It's great to have new CSS features and small JavaScript to help add typographic details, such as special letters, paragraphs and columns, but then of course there are still issues with different browsers' rendering, which can really be a pain. We talk to our clients about what browsers their audience are using, and discuss what features we can use and what the fallback will be; these are, of course, 'progressive enhancements' and it is fun to use them.

4.67–4.68 | Danish Maritime Museum
New identity and website for the Danish Maritime Museum. The website home page features a playful and unusual scrolling system to access the latest stories about the Museum's development.

Industry perspective → Workshop IV

When specifying type sizes and layout dimensions on the Web, do you use a particular measurement system and if so, why?

No. Personally, I think that there are a lot of designers who are obsessed with measurements that have to add up using mathematical solutions, but I think it's really rubbish! It is all about how something looks. Of course, you need to test it a lot in the browsers to see how things look because the line height and stuff varies so much from Photoshop to the browser.

Are there any future technical developments that you are looking forward to that will make a difference to how and what you design?

Retina! It is such a pleasure to not worry about the blurriness; everything looks so sharp and good on retina displays. Also, you can really feel that the browsers are getting up to speed with handling fonts and that is really interesting.

We have started to use fonts for icons and graphics on sites. We are going to become less image based and more vector based.

That's really interesting – so you're creating your own fonts full of icons for various websites?

Yes, it was a plan we talked about for a site we just launched, but it didn't happen this time. It's not a new approach – I think Microsoft did this back in 1995. Yes, it really makes sense now with the retina displays.

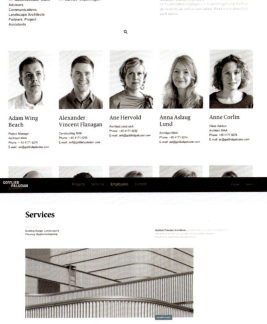

4.69–4.72 | Adapting to different window viewport sizes
The website for Gottlieb Paludan Architects features beautiful typographic details, such as illuminated letters and a clever layout, that adapts to different window viewport sizes.

Workshop IV:
Semi precious

This workshop will give you the opportunity to improve your typographic skills by creating a design for an eBook magazine. Thumbnail sketches for this project may take just 60 minutes though a fully rendered mock-up in Adobe Photoshop or Illustrator would easily take three hours or more depending on the time you have available.

Background

The explosion in interest for portable and high-powered eBook readers, such as Amazon's Kindle and Apple's iPad, have reignited interest in the art of book and magazine design. Now, magazines can be both beautiful and updateable in portable formats.

According to Amazon, eBook sales in 2012 were more than the total combined for hardback and paperbacks; for every 100 physical books sold, customers downloaded 114 eBooks. In comparison, digital magazine sales are much more modest according to a report by Alliance for Audited Media; digital editions of consumer magazines accounted for around 2.5% of all US magazine sales in 2012; however, this was up from 1% in 2011.

Brief

Your brief is to design a new digital eBook magazine called *Semi Precious* that shows how beautiful typography and layout can be on screen. The magazine is called *Semi Precious* because that is what many magazines strive to be: desirable, important, valuable but ultimately time limited and replaceable.

The term 'semi precious' is an oxymoron, which is a figure of speech that means the conjoining of contradictory terms, such as 'a deafening silence' or 'daily special'. The magazine will use oxymorons to theme its contents – for example, an article called 'American English' could be about a new novel set in England by an American author.

You must design a masthead for the magazine, a cover illustration, contents page and an article. All illustrations must be typographically based.

Oxymoron list

American English	Anxious patient
Bittersweet	Cold sweat
Daily special	Dark star
Elected king	Essential luxury
Eternal life	Fire water
Front end	Genuine fake
Half full	Homework
Lightweight	Open secret
Original copy	Player coach
Political promise	Prison life
Quiet scream	Random logic
Real fantasy	Rock opera
Safety hazard	Second best
Small fortune	Smart bomb
Traffic flow	True lies
Virtual reality	War games

Choose any of the above oxymorons to help you create a content page and provide a topic for your article.

With each of the following steps, start with pencil and paper before moving to a computer to visualize your designs.

Step 1 – Masthead
The masthead is the title of a newspaper or magazine; in web design it refers to the top of the web page where the logo and global navigation usually reside. You should design a masthead for *Semi Precious* that also includes the tagline: 'A contemporary classic magazine'. The masthead may appear on both the front cover and contents page.

Step 2 – Cover
Design a cover for your first issue of *Semi Precious*. The cover illustration must be typographically based. You may decide to use the oxymoron article titles or the names of people, places or subjects featured in your illustration – it is completely up to you.

Step 3 – Contents
Select no more than a dozen oxymorons to form the basis of your content page. Look at magazines to see what information is usually included in the contents.
At this stage, you might want to consider the resolution of your display; for example, 768x1024 pixels for a portrait is a common resolution for tablet devices.

Step 4 – Article
For the body text, you may want to add a placeholder *lorem ipsum* text rather than create, find or adapt an appropriate article. You can generate *lorem ipsum* text by using *www.lipsum.com*. Your article will have a number of additional typographic elements to consider:

Headline – title of the article
Deck – short summary of the feature article (optional)
Byline – author credit
Lead – first paragraph designed to engage the reader
Caption – description of image or illustration with credit
Folio – page number, magazine name, issue and date.

115

4.73–4.77 | Workshop examples
(Designed by Santosh Rudra)
Top: Masthead.
Middle: Cover and contents.
Bottom: Article.

The design of layouts is an activity that designers and non-designers appear to do instinctively. Whether by intuition or luck, successful compositions have usually satisfied a number of aesthetic and hierarchical considerations. However, our twenty-first century understanding of digital layouts and the grid systems that underpin them is a complex business. It relies on a sophisticated appreciation of compositional experimentation, psychology, rationalism, technical limitations and the principles of interaction.

This chapter will shed light on these considerations through an exploration of design history, principles of composition and models of grid layout. It will also explain accepted conventions and standards for design layout across a number of digital media and interactive applications – from online publishing and banner ad design to digital television.

Grids and layout

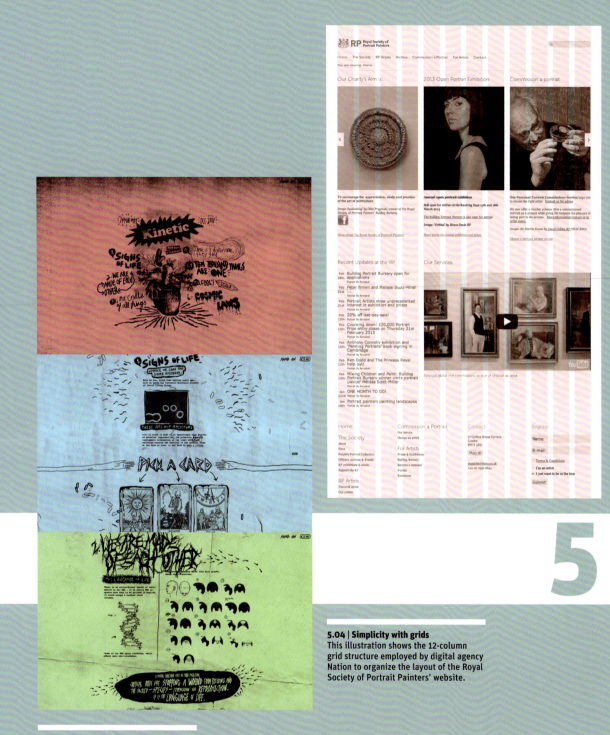

5

5.04 | Simplicity with grids
This illustration shows the 12-column
grid structure employed by digital agency
Nation to organize the layout of the Royal
Society of Portrait Painters' website.

5.01–5.03 | Complexity without grids
Kinetic's own website uses a non-grid
based graphic user interface that
incorporates parallax scrolling to promote
their creativity. To see more visit:
kinetic.com.sg

A short history

While the use of grid systems to organize and structure layout can be traced back to classical times, the last 150 years have witnessed significant developments in our understanding of composition, with creative endeavour broadly shifting between periods of artistic expression and formal rationalism. It is the epoch that this section will focus on.

The minimalist mantra of 'form follows function' that we use today owes a debt to the aspirations of artist and writer William Morris and the Art and Crafts Movement, which began in 1860s Britain. This movement was a reaction to the values of the Victorian era, which many felt had become stymied by the mass production of overly decorative and often poorly designed products.

Their philosophy manifested itself in well-crafted forms of simplicity and a new use of asymmetrical design. In layout and typography, the movement stimulated highly stylized publications, including Aubrey Beardsley's *The Yellow Book* and a number of gothic typefaces that are still in common use today: Copperplate Gothic (1901) and Franklin Gothic (1903).

Although the Arts and Crafts Movement influenced the intellectual development of design rationalism, modern design layout's visual expression was inspired by later developments in poetry and art. The work of leading poets, such as Guillaume Apollinaire and E.E. Cummings, used layout and typography to enhance creative expression; their work is an early example of 'concrete' poetry, where the typographical arrangement of letters and words is integral to its meaning.

5.05 | William Morris (1834–1896)
An artist and designer closely associated with the Arts and Crafts Movement.

5.06 | An early example of concrete poetry
A calligramme by French poet and writer Guillaume Apollinaire: an early example of concrete poetry where typographic layout is intrinsic to the interpretation of text.

5.07 | De Stijl magazine
Geometric abstraction, the first cover design of *De Stijl* magazine (1917), designed by Dutch artist and architect Theo van Doesburg (1883–1931).

The First World War stirred a desire for political and social change, which is embodied in Dutch De Stijl, Russian Constructivism and Swiss-based Dadaist art. These movements used bold compositions of colour, shape, typography and photomontage to communicate powerful and symbolic revolutionary messages.

These three movements had an important influence on the philosophy and teaching of the newly formed Bauhaus in Weimar Germany from 1919. Under the directorship of architect Walter Gropius, this arts and crafts school was liberal and modernist in outlook, highly valuing experimentation and rationalism. Constructivists El Lissitzky and László Moholy-Nagy, and De Stijl's founder Theo van Doesburg, were just a few of the leading artists, designers and intellectuals who taught there; they encouraged experimentation with asymmetrical compositions and photomontage.

When the first Weimar Bauhaus exhibition was staged in 1923, it had a profound effect on a young German typographer called Jan Tschichold, who was inspired by their experimental layout and typography. Tschichold went on to publish a number of influential works, including his seminal book *Die Neue Typographie* in 1928, in which he advocated a new minimal and functional aesthetic for typography and grid layout.

The Bauhaus' modernist approach was spreading. In London in 1930, Beatrice Warde published a landmark essay on typography called the 'The Crystal Goblet' and gave a speech at St Brides, the Typographers' Guild, in which she called for increased transparency in typography and printing. The Bauhaus' thinking was not universally welcomed; its liberal and radical views were perceived as dangerous by the political right-wing, and in 1933 the Bauhaus School was forced to close due to mounting nationalist pressure. However, this only widened the reach of ideas, as its teaching staff moved to Switzerland, Britain and the USA where they began successful design practices. In 1937, László Moholy-Nagy was invited to set up a new design school in Chicago, which was named the New Bauhaus.

5.08 | Foto-Qualität, IX.1.2
Produced in 1926 by Hungarian painter and photographer László Moholy-Nagy (1895–1946)

5.09 | 'The Woman Without A Name' film poster
'Die Frau ohne Namen' (1927) was designed by German typographer Jan Tschichold (1902–1974).

Modernist ideas continued to have a major influence on design layout after The Second World War, particularly through the formalization of corporate identity systems. From the 1970s, post-modern ideas can be seen in the work of Wolfgang Weingart and April Greiman, which then continued at a pace with the explosion of 'deconstructed' graphic design in the late 1980s and early 1990s, exemplified in the designs of Katherine McCoy and the typography of Barry Deck.

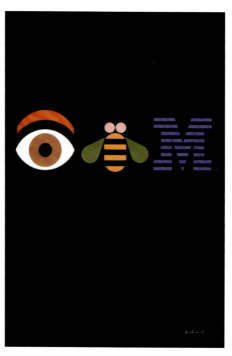

5.11 | Eye-Bee-M poster
This poster for IBM (1981) by American graphic designer, Paul Rand (1914–1996), was a more playful and ephemeral piece of corporate communication, in contrast to the enduring design philosophy incorporated in his brand identity work for IBM between the mid 1950s and early 1990s.

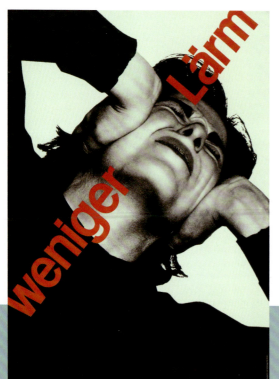

5.10 | Weniger Lärm poster
Weniger Lärm or 'Stop Noise Pollution' in English, was a public service poster (1960) designed by Swiss graphic designer and teacher Josef Müller-Brockmann (1914–1996).

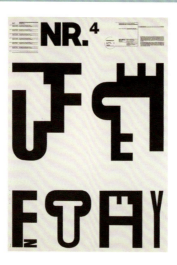

5.12 | Typographic process, Nr 4.
Typographic signs (1971–72) by Swiss graphic designer Wolfgang Weingart (1941–).

5.13 | *Wet* magazine
Cover (1979) by American graphic designer April Greiman (1948–).

This modernist approach, known as the 'International Typographic Style', was taken up by a new generation of designers, including Otl Aicher, Josef Müller-Brockmann, Massimo Vignelli and Paul Rand. It was highly influential in the field of graphic design both before and long after The Second World War as its systematic approach to design layout became the foundation of many corporate identity programmes.

The modernist view that design should strive for objectivity remained unchallenged until the late 1980s when leading designers began to use the work of French philosophers Jacques Derrida and Roland Barthes to critique their practice. Derrida's theory of 'deconstruction' asks how the representation of an object, product or idea becomes its perceived reality. In the case of design layout, does an idea's presentation through image and typography become its reality in the reader's eyes?

Moreover, Barthes' 'codes theory' asserts the importance of the reader over the writer in the creation of meaning. These theories and critiquing stimulated a 'post-modern' era of graphic design, which was often articulated through highly stylized layered designs recognizably different from the simplicity of modernism. Just as in concrete poetry, content and its communication through design had once again become inseparable.

In the latter half of the 1990s, deconstruction had become an overused aesthetic style rather than a tired intellectual argument. It was also unsuitable for the needs of a new challenge for design layout borne of technology rather than ideological revolution. The birth of the Internet and the ubiquity of interactive devices required a more functional design philosophy to meet the needs of individual users. Technology had given a worldwide audience 24/7 access to online media, but just as importantly, it has also given individuals the ability to create and distribute their own content, too. For designers, this presented new creative and technical challenges for design layout to resolve. Now, designers working in interactive media are increasingly required to design attractive and functional templates and style sheets for content creators to use, and the plethora of new devices and technological platforms require both greater technical knowledge and behavioural understanding in order to create dynamic compositions that work across them all.

For further reading on the development of grid systems and graphic design history, the following books are highly recommended: Ellen Lupton's *Thinking with Type: A Critical Guide for Designers, Writers, Editors and Students* (2010) and Timothy Samara's *Making and Breaking the Grid: A Graphic Design Layout Workshop* (2005).

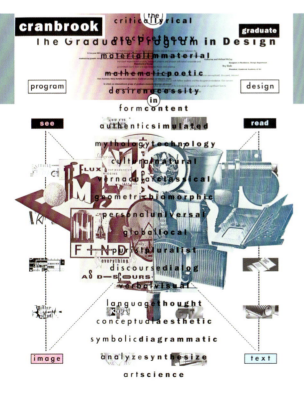

5.14 | Deconstructivist graphic design
'See Read' poster for Cranbrook Graduate Design (1989) by Katherine McCoy (1945–) shows a collage of recent student work overlaid with opposing design values. This is an example of deconstructivist graphic design.

5.15 | Template Gothic
Designed in 1990 by American typographer Barry Deck (1962–), this seminal typeface of the 1990s represented the distorted imperfections of the post-modern era. (Poster designed by Matt Chea).

Principles of composition

The composition of design layouts is a challenging, but rewarding activity for a designer. It requires years of practice to hone our skills so that we can create order and harmony out of a collection of disparate parts. When we design screen layouts for interactive and digital media, it is important to remember that our primary focus is to communicate messages and deliver information to the user, rather than it being purely an exercise in creative experimentation.

The following principles draw heavily on Gestalt theories of perception, an appreciation of the Golden Section and the Rule of Thirds to help organize and structure visual elements. In the process, values that help order and create hierarchy will also be highlighted.

5.16–5.18 | Extending the Cervélo brand
Cervélo, the industry leader in bike engineering, engaged digital agency, Reactive, to design and develop their new website, which features many strong visuals that provide excellent examples of composition principles. The considered design very successfully extends the Cervélo brand to a digital platform. The site structure is clear, intuitive and engaging, enabling the user to fully explore effortlessly.

Balance

Balance refers to the placement and distribution of elements on a page. When balance is achieved, the composition has a pleasing harmony and stability. This sense of satisfactory equilibrium can be explained through the Gestalt Law of Symmetry, which states that our minds perceive unconnected elements as symmetrical when they can be formed around a centre point to make one coherent shape.

However, satisfying layout is not always something that is desirable. Symmetrical can also mean dull. When a layout is unbalanced, it creates a natural movement and tension. For this reason, asymmetrical layouts have often been a compositional preference for modernist designers, who want to create layouts with direction and energy.

Shape and space

Shapes are commonly used elements in composition; however, they take more time for the brain to process than colour or size because they have to be interpreted and identified. The Gestalt Laws of Closure and Similarity are applicable to shape recognition and layout.

The Law of Closure applies when a shape is not whole, in which case we mentally fill the gap and perceive it complete. The Law of Similarity applies when shapes appear similar and so the brain perceives them as a group or pattern. This is particularly useful for information design as elements of a similar visual nature can be segmented to form groups with a simple change of colour.

Positive and negative spaces are commonly used terms by designers when composing layouts, creating logos or detailing lines of type. Positive space refers to the figure or object that appears to exist (such as a letterform or silhouette of an image), whereas negative refers to the space that surrounds it.

Size and scale

Size is an excellent variable for creating order and hierarchy; larger elements draw our attention more than smaller ones so we automatically assign them greater importance. This is why bold text appears more important than regular text.

Comparative size and scale are not just good for assigning importance in composition. Scaling images and text is also useful for representing interaction – for example, application icons scale up when rolled over in Mac OS X or images appear larger when highlighted in iTunes.

Colour and contrast: red is used to highlight important 'calls to action', such as user login, as well as important navigation elements, such as the next image.

Position and placement: the row of dots underneath the main images is perceived as a group, so are the three images and associated columns of text at the bottom. Proximity is a key factor in mentally grouping elements.

JAKUB MACEL

Jakub is a full time Cervélo employee, triathlete and Cervélo sponsored athlete.

Like 0 | SUBSCRIBE

Explore More

JAKUB MACEL

Jakub, or "Jakes" as we call him, works full time at Cervélo as a Customer Service and Technical Rep. When Jakub isn't helping our customers out on the phones, you will most likely catch him at the many Triathlon events we attend, offering his services to make sure your bike is race-ready before check-in. Jakes is an age grouper athlete, who became a Cervélo sponsored athlete this year.

Jakes set his eye on qualifying for Kona this year and we are happy to say that he will be racing his P5 at Ironman 70.3 Worlds in Vegas and Ironman Worlds Championships in Kona. More on him shortly.

Race Calendar

Date	Event
09/09/2012	Ironman 70.3 World Championships, Vegas
10/13/2012	Ironman World Championship, Kona, Hawaii

RELATED BIKES

P5

MACEL ON TWITTER ›

EXPLORE MORE

Mary Beth Ellis's post-race wisdom

US Champion, Mary Beth Ellis shares some post race wisdom after Ironman New York.

Tyler does Bermuda proud at the Olympics

Tyler Butterfield's fastest bike splits during the Olympics

Laurel Wassner on Ironman New York

Professional triathlete Laurel Wassner speaks about what motivated her to do an Ironman

---

P SERIES

Cervélo Triathlon/Time trial bicycles have won more pro races than any other, and they are by far the most popular bicycles at Ironman and time trial events for athletes of all levels.

REVOLUTIONARY AERODYNAMICS

Like 7 | SUBSCRIBE

TRIATHLON & TIME TRIAL

These bikes are confident in their #1 position in the 'superbike' category. Cervélo triathlon/time trial bicycles have won more pro races than any other, and they are by far the most popular bicycles at Ironman and time trial events for athletes of all levels. Boasting revolutionary aerodynamic designs developed through our extensive testing and experience, Cervélo has designed the most copied triathlon and TT bicycles in history. Once you ride one, you'll immediately feel the lightning speed, but also the perfect fit and comfort needed to sustain your aero position during long distance races, or to tackle the toughest sprints.

How did we make a superbike 'simply faster'?

The P5 features the most aerodynamic frameset and aerobars, but speed hasn't come at the expense of simplicity. Built with non-proprietary components, we have made this bike easy to set up, easy to adjust, and easy to travel with—no more searching out specialty shops on the road or carrying extra tools. It also features an aero hydraulic brake, maximizing speed management with zero maintenance. Last but not least, we made sure it offers the widest possible fit range and innovative hydration and storage solutions. Easy to handle, easy to live with, and easy to push to top speeds.

Space: we recognize the abstract shape as an é because we mentally fill in the missing space to form the letter shape. This is referred to as the Law of Closure.

The P5 Six

KEY TECHNOLOGIES

Shape recognition takes longer for the brain to process; it is quicker to read the word 'brake' than it is to identify the shape of the brake.

P5 Fit

Newly engineered geometry developed to accommodate an extensive range of fit coordinates.

COMFORT, SIMPLICITY

P5 Aerobar

The world's fastest and best fitting aerobar, with unmatched adjustability and 100% hidden cables.

AERO, COMFORT, SIMPLICITY

P5 Magura Brake

High compatibility to fit all wheels, and an extremely user-friendly quick release system at the hub.

SIMPLICITY

Balance is created by centre aligning these typographic elements underneath three images that in turn compositionally balance around the centre column.

P SERIES

P2   P3   P5

Scale creates hierarchy. The large images above assume more importance than these small thumbnails.

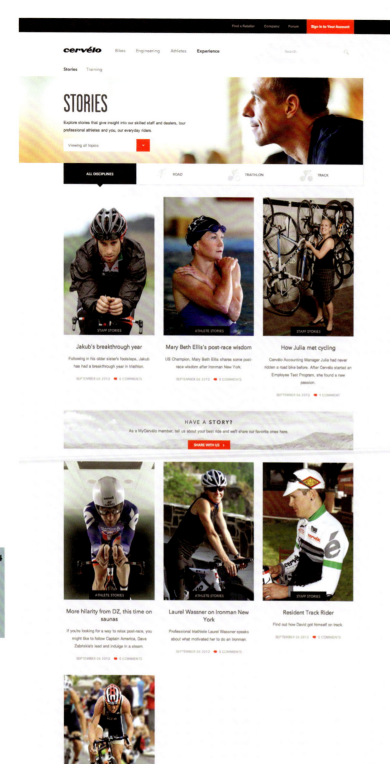

Position and placement

We tend to perceive elements that are close together as a group; this perception is known as the Law of Proximity. Interestingly, the uniformity of shape or distance isn't a prerequisite for this law to work.

The visual placement of elements on the screen is subject to learnt as well as natural order. In Western cultures, people read from top left to bottom right so if all compositional elements were of a similar size, the elements nearest the top left would assume the most importance. This emphasizes the need to understand your audience, as this scenario would be different for Chinese, Islamic and Semitic users, who naturally read from right to left.

Colour and contrast

Colour is a key value in composition as differences in colour hue and saturation alter the perceived focus and importance of compositional elements. Although there is no inherent order in colour choice, colours with higher hue, saturation and brightness will appear more important than those with more muted tones.

Colour is also useful in identifying similarities and differences between elements. As with shape, it can be used to associate and unify unrelated elements.

Unlike colour, contrast can create an order of importance. Elements with the greatest contrast against their background will appear more dominant if all other factors are equal. Text in a composition needs to be legible against its background to provide an acceptable reading experience. The World Wide Web Consortium (W3C) provides accessibility guidelines on colour contrast and there are many online resources to help you assess it, too (see Useful resources section, page 203).

5.19 | Rule of thirds
This layout breaks neatly into thirds to display the stories and divides further for the footer elements at the base of the page layout.

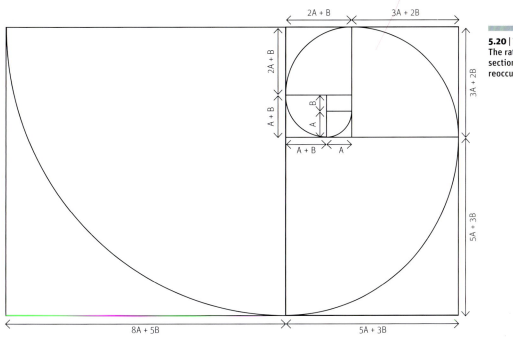

Golden section

The golden section is a mathematical ratio found throughout nature that has been used since ancient times for its aesthetically pleasing proportions. Its formula and use can be traced in the geometry of Euclid and Pythagoras, the Roman architecture of Vitruvius and the Renaissance illustration of Leonardo Da Vinci. More recently, it has influenced contemporary design; from our ISO paper sizes and Jan Tschichold's grid layout proportions, to the dimensions of widescreen televisions and even the iPod.

The golden section or ratio expressed in algebraic term:

$$\frac{a+b}{a} = \frac{a}{b} \overset{\text{def}}{=} \Phi$$

In simpler terms, the $a+b$ is to a what a is to b.

The Fibonacci sequence, which is closely related to the proportions of the golden section or golden ratio, makes it simpler to see the relationship between the two proportions: each number in the sequence is derived from the addition of its two predecessors:

Fibonacci sequence: 0, 1, 1, 2, 3, 5, 8, 13, 21, 34, 55, 89, 144...

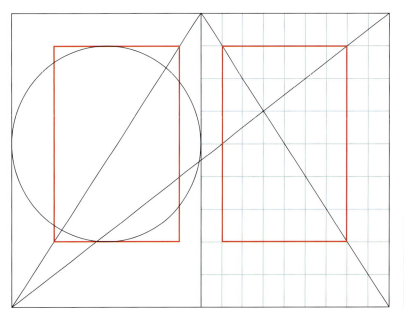

125

Rule of thirds

While the golden section provides insight into the most pleasing aesthetic proportions for design layout, it would provide most interactive designers with number crunching headaches when applying it to design. To make things simpler, many designers use the rule of thirds to help create compositions.

The rule suggests that a composition should be divided into thirds by using two horizontal and two vertical guidelines to make nine equally sized parts. The most important elements should then be placed at the intersections to create compositions with the most dynamic and visual interest.

The following section will take these principles further by introducing the importance of creating a grid structure to underpin our compositional layouts.

What are grids?

Grids provide the skeletal structure that supports design to deliver content. A well-designed grid system for a website or application will appear invisible to the end user. At most, there will be an innate efficiency and perhaps pleasure in using it, reaffirming their choice of visiting this site or downloading this application.

Grid systems provide visual coherence on a website and help organize page elements. Beyond the navigation elements, grids also provide consistency and logic when drilling down through layers of complex information and media content.

More than adding uniformity, grids help important messages to stand out by establishing a visual hierarchy of information. Grids, in conjunction with Cascading Style Sheets (CSS), provide designers and users with the tools to create flexible and dynamic layouts. Well-designed grid systems give designers and users the ability to create a variety of layouts quickly and efficiently while remaining consistent.

The *960.gs* grid system

The *960.gs* is perhaps the most used grid system in web design today. It is named after its width of 960 pixels that neatly fits into a 1024x768 pixel display without the need for horizontal scrolling. This grid is credited to Nathan Smith, an American designer and developer, who created the system to streamline his web development process. There are two main variants: the 12-column and the 16-column grid versions.

The 12-column grid is particularly useful as both symmetrical and asymmetrical compositions can easily be created using the same grid. For example, an image and a text box each spanning six columns can be placed side by side to create a balanced composition. Alternatively, an asymmetrical composition can also be created – for example, a navigation panel spanning four columns adjacent to a text box with in-line images spanning eight columns; this example follows the 'rule of thirds' composition principle.

For further online guidance on grid systems, look at the following websites:

960.gs

cssgrid.net

designinfluences.com/fluid960gs

semantic.gs

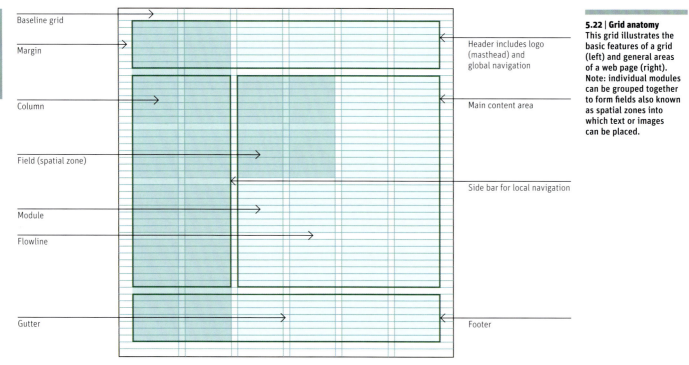

Baseline grid

Margin

Column

Field (spatial zone)

Module

Flowline

Gutter

Header includes logo (masthead) and global navigation

Main content area

Side bar for local navigation

Footer

5.22 | Grid anatomy
This grid illustrates the basic features of a grid (left) and general areas of a web page (right). Note: individual modules can be grouped together to form fields also known as spatial zones into which text or images can be placed.

5.23–5.26 | 12-column grid system

The Royal Society of Portrait Painters' website designed by Nation is based on a 12-column 960 grid system. The 12 columns are overlaid in red so that you can appreciate how the layouts are formed using this grid system.

Screen size and layout

There are no definitive standards for screen resolution or browser window sizes because the designer has little control over the screen on which pages are viewed nor influence on the user who may resize their browser window at will. This may seem frustrating to some designers when embarking on web-based projects, but it is no different from a newspaper designer sighing at the sight of their beautiful front page layout folded several times for a commuter's reading convenience.

What web designers are able to do is optimize their designs for the best possible viewing experience. According to web browser statistics published by W3Schools, over 85% of people view web pages on monitors with screen resolutions in excess of 1024x768 pixels.

For web designers who once had to cater for users with 800x600 pixel displays, screen resolution is much less of a problem. The main concern is making sure a layout works for the extremes of a 27-inch (68.5-cm) monitor and a 4-inch (10-cm) smartphone.

Mobile

As with computer monitors, the size and resolution of mobile devices can vary hugely. The latest Apple iPad and Amazon Kindle Fire tablets have higher resolutions than many desktop computers.

A lack of screen standardization means that designers and software developers have adopted common screen sizes and technical solutions to create the best possible viewing experience for users.

These common screen sizes work with three basic categories of mobile device: **feature phones**, smartphones and tablets. Each has different screen sizes, navigation methods and screen orientations from desktop and laptop PCs.

The differences in navigation method between devices with their own established patterns of use are commonly referred to as **User Experience Design Patterns** or 'UX' patterns for short.

Screen resolution

The following table shows the most common screen resolutions for design layouts with maximum web browser window sizes in brackets where applicable. On monitor screens, the browser navigation bar and menu reduce the vertical screen space available by about 150 pixels and the scroll bar reduces the width by about 20 pixels. Note: tablets and phones generally rely on touch gestures rather than bars for scrolling.

Popular screen resolutions

Monitor resolution[1]	Tablet	Smartphone	Feature phone
1024x768 (1000x620)	1024x600	320x480	**240x320**
1280x1024 (1260x875)	**1024x768**	**480x800**	
1440x900 (1420x750)	1280x800	1136x640[3]	
1600x1200 (1580x1050)	2048x1536[2]		

Resolutions in **bold** represent the most common screen sizes used by designers.

1   These figures represent common monitor resolutions; however, resolutions can go much higher with some 30-inch (76-cm) monitors having screen resolutions of 2560x1600.
2   iPad 4th generation with retina display.
3   iPhone 5 with retina display.

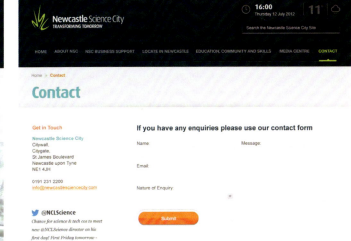

Why is Newcastle a Science City?

Newcastle was designated as one of
six UK Science Cities in 2005 in

Ageing & Health

Recognising the benefits of better understanding the ageing process.

5.27–28 | Newcastle Science City
This website, designed by Komodo Digital, has two separate websites for desktop and mobile viewing so that differences in both screen resolutions and user experience patterns can be carefully designed for each medium.

5.29–5.31 | Mobile design for Science City
The layout is not just simplified for mobile viewing; the navigation options are designed specifically for the size of your fingers when using a touch screen.

Newcastle was designated as one of six UK Science Cities in 2005 in recognition of the world class research being undertaken by its universities and the potential of its science industry base.

Newcastle was designated as one of six UK Science Cities in 2005 in recognition of the world class research being undertaken by its universities and the potential of its science industry base.

Newcastle was designated as one of six UK Science Cities in 2005 in recognition of the world class research being undertaken by its universities and the potential of its science industry base.

Laying out web content

In its relatively short history, web design layout has developed a widely adopted set of conventions and principles for the organization and placement of content. For designers, there is always a balance to be struck between providing the user with something that is visually exciting or stimulating and at the same time familiar and reassuring. However, when dealing with continually evolving interactive formats where the user has experienced new pleasures through year on year technological innovations, web layout has made more steady progress prioritizing familiarity and usability over creative experimentation.

Basic conventions and principles

A well-designed website has a structured layout based on a grid, making it easier for the user to appreciate the hierarchy of unambiguous and clearly labelled content.

The layout should have clear navigation with the website logo (home button) in the top left corner, with global navigation also at the top and local navigation on the left-hand side. Users do not always have their browser window maximized to full screen so essential navigation items should always be top left.

Lead the user to the content they are looking for and make sure that important content is placed near the top of the page. Users should not have to scroll to find essential content; scrolling should be used only to read more detail. Content should be grouped or broken down into scannable elements known as 'chunks', using visual breaks where appropriate.

Z- and F-layouts

The Z- and F-layouts are commonly used in web design to meet the communication needs of website owners' websites and acknowledge the scanning patterns of their users.

The Z-layout encourages the user to read the webpage in a Z-shaped path taking in the website's identity, navigation structure and high-level content before finally resting on a 'Call to Action' (CTA), normally in the shape of a button or link. A 'Call to Action' is a prompt and is an essential inbound marketing technique that tries to turn a user into a customer by funnelling them down a particular path on a website; for example, to purchase a product or sign-up for a service.

The F-shape layout is based on an eye-tracking study by the Nielsen Norman Group (2006), which suggests that users scanning information tend to read in an F-shaped pattern; so important information should be placed on or near this established path. In the study, users first horizontally scanned information at the top of the screen, then made a second horizontal sweep a little further down and finally took their time to read vertically down the content on the left-hand side of the screen. It must be noted that this study focused on heavy designs and search results so users were scanning rather than actively reading chosen content, which would affect their reading pattern.

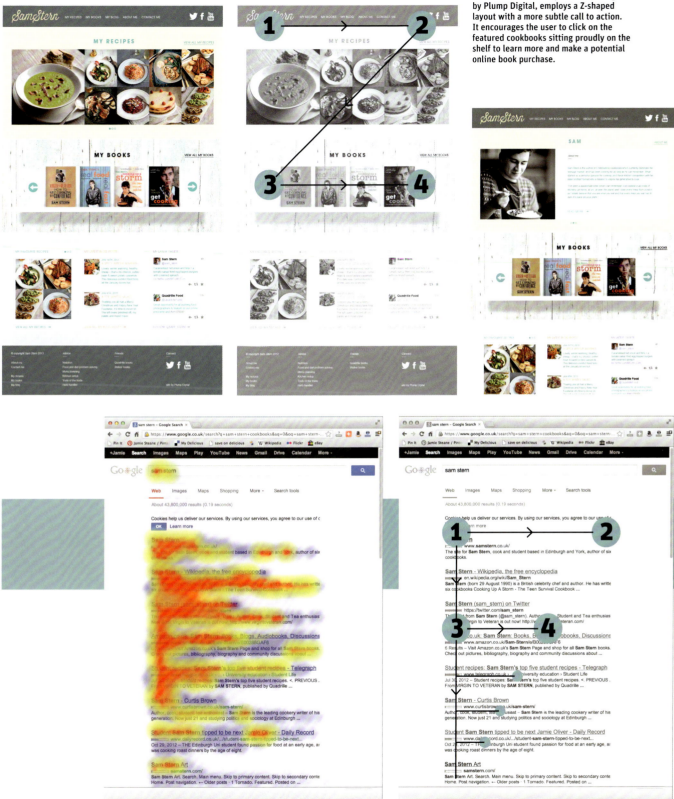

5.32–5.34 | Z-layout
The Sam Stern cookery website, designed by Plump Digital, employs a Z-shaped layout with a more subtle call to action. It encourages the user to click on the featured cookbooks sitting proudly on the shelf to learn more and make a potential online book purchase.

5.35–5.36 | F-layout
This heat map illustrates the typical F-shape pattern created using eye-tracking software when users scan search results.

Fluid, responsive and adaptive design layouts

Website design has made huge leaps in progress since the first graphic Web browsers were introduced in 1993. The proliferation of Web 2.0 technologies has enabled greater social interaction and self-publishing opportunities that require designers to consider layouts that best support them. In the last couple of years, designers have witnessed a long anticipated Holy Grail – full control over the layout and typography, thanks to the combination of HTML5, CCS3 and web fonts.

These technologies, together with a requirement to support web browsing on numerous devices, have lead to new approaches in design layout. These approaches and their implications for future design layout will now be explained.

Fixed and fluid layouts

Fixed layouts have a specified width within which elements such as columns, type and images may also have fixed sizes. The main advantage of this system is that layouts are easier to implement and are consistent for every browser. The main disadvantage is to usability; the design may require horizontal scrolling and zooming based on the width of the browser window and screen resolution.

5.37 | Sunderland College website
An example of an adaptive web design, by Komodo Digital, that contains breakpoints at which the design layout changes depending on the browser's window size.

5.38–5.42 | Adaptive design
Side-by-side layouts show how the design alters for different viewport sizes: 1024, 768, 600, 480 and 320 widths.

In contrast, fluid or 'liquid' layouts scale to the size of your browser window by using percentages rather than pixel or point measurements to define the size of type, images and other on-screen elements. The chief benefit of fluid layouts is that they are more user-friendly. However, lack of control over what the user sees may also cause the website to appear oversized on large high-resolution monitors.

Fluid grids and responsive web design

A responsive website uses a design that scales and rearranges page elements based on the width of the browser window. This can be achieved through the use of fluid grids and images and the @media **CSS3** query that lets the designer interrogate the width of the user's browser window. A fluid grid allows the designer to specify at what browser width a layout changes; these arbitrary widths are more commonly known as 'breakpoints' and are based on how the designer wants the layout to appear on different screen sizes, also known as '**viewports**'; for example, 320, 480, 600, 768, 1024, 1200 pixels.

For example, if the width is greater than 768 pixels, you may want a three-column grid. However, at less than 320 pixels it may just have one column. Using a responsive web design approach, users will always see a layout that is suitable for their screen and window size.

Progress enhancement and adaptive design

Progressive enhancement is a web design strategy based on the principle that every user receives a basic content and functionality, but those with more advanced browser features and bandwidth receive a more enhanced experience.

Adaptive design is the combination of responsive web design and progressive enhancement to deliver a web experience that adjusts to both the form and function of a user's web browsing capabilities.

5.43–5.44 | Red Bull Music Academy Radio

This responsive design by Edenspiekermann is a new online radio experience that puts music and people front and centre. It features today's essential music makers and DJs, the best new tunes, and all the festival moments that really matter. With the new *rbmaradio.com* and native apps, users can now easily browse through thousands of interviews, mixes and live recordings that they won't find anywhere else on the Web.

5.45–5.46 | Agile development
Edenspiekermann changed the way that the Red Bull Music Academy thought about its service and how it's developed. They applied **agile** methodologies to allow for rapid product development, frequent changes and early adoption of upcoming trends and standards.

5.47 | Content layout
The new design puts emphasis on the presentation of each individual show, beautifully organized in a hierarchical and responsive grid system.

RBMA Radio *The best music selection on the web*

SHOWS LISTS LATEST

Interviews & Features · Interviews & Features

Donald Byrd

Still feels like loving you today. A two-hour homage to one of the finest musical souls in jazz history. Donald Byrd, rest in peace brother.

Grooverider
From 80s warehouse raves to the hardcore continuum and beyond.

Live Recordings

Visionquest
Seth Troxler and his crew captured live in Panama.

Milton Nascimento
A true musical innovator and one of Brazil's most distinct voices: The life and times of Milton Nascimento as told by the man himself.

Skream
The magnetic man they call Skream with a two-hour-plus lesson in bass-heavy club music across the board. Live from Berlin's CTM Festival.

Acid Mothers Temple
Where the whopping wild freaks live: AMT mastermind Kawabata Makoto breaks down the story behind Japan's ever-mutating space-rock commune.

Fatima Al Qadiri
From Kuwait to NYC: Multi-faceted composer and sonic adventurer Fatima Al Qadiri picks a fine selection of jams that keep her going.

Festival · Themes · Clubs

UP NEXT ON: HIGHLIGHTS

| Redshape | Sébastien Tellier | Nguzunguzu | Marc 'MK' Kinchen | Sly & Robbie | DOOM |
| Fireside Chat | Fireside Chat | Sónar Sessions 2012 | Live at U Street Music H... | Fireside Chat | Live at Són |

Jah Wobble
Fireside Chat

59:32 · CHANNELS

135

Television screen layout and standards

Although moving pictures and sounds are the primary means of communication, grids and screen layout still perform an important role on television. Screen layouts are used for a wide variety of duties, from programme titling and news information graphics through to interactive television content and DVD menu systems. Designers working in television need to become familiar with its standards and conventions to create practical designs.

Screen layout considerations

There are noticeable differences in composition between television and other media such as print or web; for technical reasons, television generally uses less complex layouts with bolder typography. Television is a relatively low-quality medium with pixel densities often falling below 72dpi on large TV screens so less images and text will fit on screen.

Furthermore, all text should always be placed within the middle 80% of the screen called the 'title safe area' to guarantee that it won't be cropped due to over-scanning or individual users widescreen settings. Similarly, important moving images should be kept in the middle 90%, called the 'action safe area'.

To reiterate advice given in the previous chapter, type also needs to be large: generally a minimum 24pt for body text and 60pts for headlines so that they can be read from viewing distances of at least ten feet (three metres).

Broadcasting standards

While Digital Video Broadcasting (DVB) is an internationally accepted broadcast standard for the future delivery of high-definition digital television, it is likely that longer established regional broadcast standards will continue for some time to come. There are three widely used regional standards: PAL, NTSC and SECAM.

PAL (Phase Alternating Line) is used throughout Europe, South America, Central Asia and Australia.

NTSC (National Television Standards Committee) is used in North America, Japan and Korea.

SECAM (Séquentiel couleur à mémoire (sequential colour with memory)) is used in France, parts of Africa, the Middle East and Russia.

Although television graphics are commonly created at 72dpi, these standards have different image sizes, aspect ratios, **frame rates** and even colour gamut ranges.

The following table shows some of the most common standards and formats for PAL and NTSC. SECAM is not shown here as it is similar to PAL in terms of dimension and frame rates.

Action safe area

Title safe area

5.48 | Working with safety areas
This interactive menu design for Video Jukebox was designed to work within the PAL standard definition. Video Jukebox is a very early example of interactive MPEG video compilation (1995). The playful interface by Jamie Steane and Charles Paintin uses a futuristic CD player metaphor to prompt user interaction.

Television screen layout and standards → Industry perspective

Common standards and formats for NTSC and PAL

Standard	Size	Dimensions in pixels	Pixel aspect ratio	Frame rate per second
NTSC	D1	720x486	0.91	29.97
NTSC	D1 Widescreen	720x486	1,21	29.97
NTSC	D1 Square pixels	720x534	1.0	29.97
NTSC	D1 Widescreen square pixels	872x534	1.0	29.97
PAL	D1/DV	720x576	1.09	25
PAL	D1/DV Widescreen	720x576	1.46	25
PAL	D1/DV Square pixels	720x576	1.0	25
PAL	D1/DV Widescreen square pixels	1050x576	1.0	25
—	HDV/HDTV	1280x720	1.0	25/29.97
—	HDV/HDTV	1920x1080	1.0	25/29.97
Digital Cinema	Film (2K)	2048x1556	1.0	24/48
Digital Cinema	Film (4K)	4096x3112	1.0	24/48

For definitions of all acronyms above, please visit the full glossary section at the back of this book (pages 200–201).

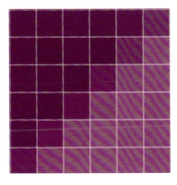
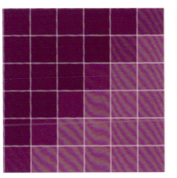
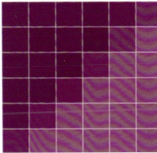
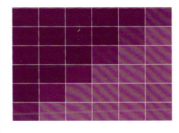

5.49–5.52 | Pixel shapes
The super enlarged illustrations show the pixel shapes based on the pixel aspect ratios listed above. From left to right: D1 Square, NTSC, PAL, PAL Widescreen.

Square and non-square pixels

The difference between televisions and computer screens is the shape of the pixels. Computers use square pixels and standard definition televisions use rectangular pixels. Looking at the table of broadcast standards, you can see the difference in pixel aspect ratios – for example, PAL **D1/DV** is 1.09 – which means that pixels are 9% wider than they are tall. In contrast, NTSC D1 has a pixel ratio of 0.91, which means that the pixels are 9% narrower than they are tall.

Note: the future is square! **High Definition Television** (**HDTV**) uses square pixels and the different regions will use common screen sizes. However, they will continue to use different frame rates.

Industry perspective:
Matt Verity, TrueView

Sector
Social networking

Digital start-up
TrueView

Core business offer
TrueView is a dating app that enables a user to build a dynamic and individual profile using everyday social media interactions, thus providing others with real-life insight to create more genuine connections with the user.

Interview with Matt Verity, Founding Partner
Matt is a London-based Senior Creative who has been working within the digital advertising industry for the past ten years. He helped to grow a small agency into a highly awarded industry leader. Matt is also active within the design community – judging awards, holding talks and running workshops.

Why do we need a new online dating service?
The online dating industry is a huge market and highly fragmented, but we found that although there are literally thousands of services out there covering every niche imaginable, they all follow the same archaic formula and are yet to align with the current shift towards mobile and social media behaviour that is now so ingrained into people's daily lives.

138

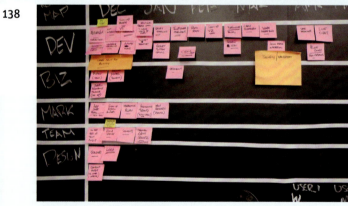

5.54–5.56 | Aspects of TrueView
TrueView development wall, agile development tasks and timeline, card sorting.

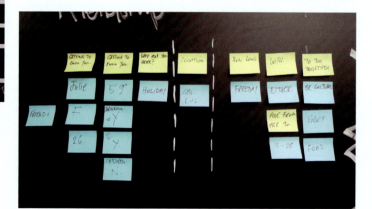

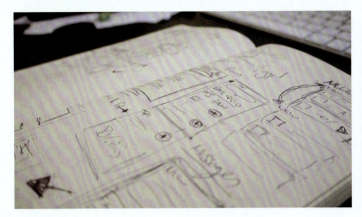
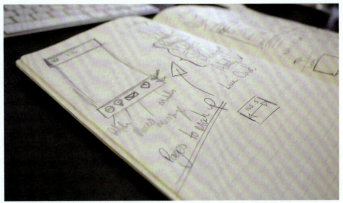

5.57–5.58 | TrueView thumbnail sketches for user interface

Why did you start with an app rather than a web-based service?

That was one of our key differentiators. The majority of services in the market started with a web-based service, and now find it very difficult to shift their model and utilize mobile effectively. The core proposition of our service was to be a service that lived alongside you, in your pocket; and that tapped into how people now access and share their lives online, through their smartphones.

When designing an app, what are the most important considerations?

Less is more. It is very easy to get over-ambitious and excited about the possibilities of how an app can look and behave. It is vital that the design is not influenced by anything other than user consideration. We have been very iterative in our approach and being in a small team has meant stripping back features because they place a thin fog over the core essence of what we want the app to do.

Are there any particular differences in layout principles between desktop and mobile?

I believe it is a completely different mindset. Desktop allows so much expression and experimentation that people accept and almost encourage it. With mobile, people have expectations and behavioural templates that they are used to. Putting a camera icon on the right when all other apps put it on the left doesn't invite applause for being different; it stops people using your app out of frustration. People use apps that make their life easier; they are a modern-day tool. If it is too complicated, people will drop it and find another tool that is much more fluid and intuitive.

139

5.59 | Site map for website and application

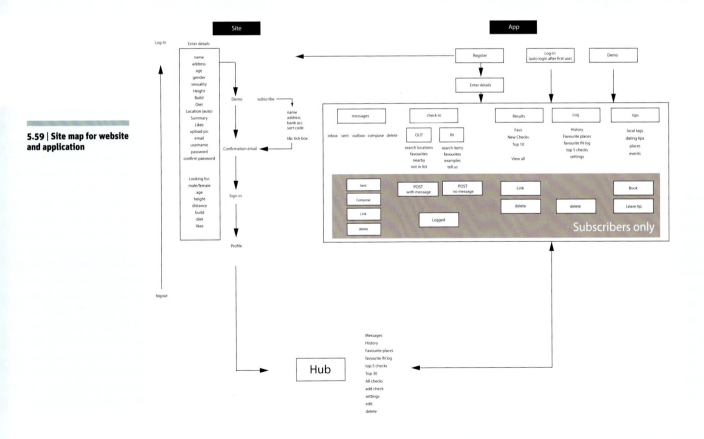

Industry perspective:
Matt Verity, TrueView

Have you had to make any compromises on any design layout?

I would say compromising has actually been another positive element to the design process. Having to really strip the ambition down helps define the core proposition of what the app does and helps filter down the design to be as efficient as possible. It is also a fine balance. The design of an app is not only about it looking good and flowing well, it is about performance and UX.

What was the hardest part of your design to get right?

That it appealed to both males and females. That it would be gender neutral, not too masculine and not too feminine. It is why I redesigned it with a new colour palette. I wouldn't say it was that hard, but it took me a while to realize that this is a product that cannot be based on assumption, but should be built on genuine insight.

Your design uses dynamic visuals such as the 'interest graph' – were these a challenge to design?

I really enjoyed how we got to this in the design. In the early stages, it wasn't fully thought through; we just knew we wanted people's information to be presented in a way that could easily be understood and used. I got very excited about your profile being a dynamic infographic and felt that it fitted perfectly with the screen real estate we were working with. So the process didn't take long; it was a pretty obvious route to take, we just needed to test various options to see which worked best.

Why did you change your global navigation from a conventional bar in your early design to a floating semi-circular selection?

As part of the design process, you obviously look at what your competitors are doing; you look at your favourite apps and you look at how you want people to use your app. For me, one of our key differentiators was going to be the design of our app. I just wanted to be the first app in the dating market to be praised for its design and UX. Changing the navigation was the most obvious way to make a bigger splash. Our app is about quick and easy updates so I wanted something that encouraged speed and ease, but that also felt friendly, fun and tactile.

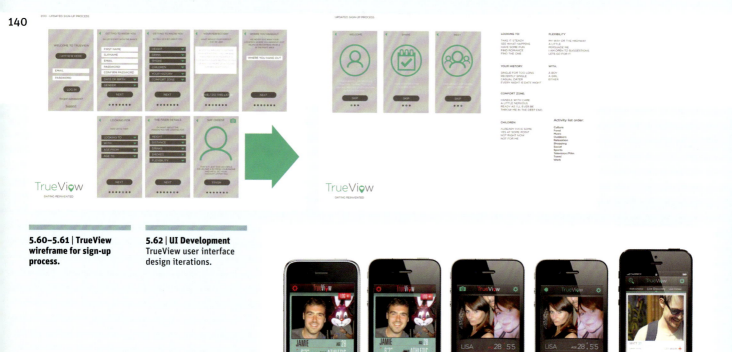

5.60–5.61 | TrueView wireframe for sign-up process.

5.62 | UI Development TrueView user interface design iterations.

Do you anticipate building a tablet or desktop version in the future?

Our app has been planned and built in a way that will mean emigrating across multiple platforms and developing a tablet version will be very easy. Although the app looks native, it is very much an HTML5 app to allow for remote updates and scaling.

If you were to give some advice on design layout for mobile what would it be?

Take your initial designs, sit with a UX specialist and be prepared for an education. The earlier the better, otherwise you have to explain to your developer why the size of everything has been doubled and moved around. Talk to the people you are designing for and get their input. It is only good design if your intended customers understand it, like it and want to use it.

Are there any technical advances in the near future that you are hoping to incorporate?

Of course, we are constantly learning from our user feedback and metrics, and researching future technical developments – it is the key to our iteration process. And by the time this book comes out, the app will be totally different again. We have some great and exciting new features planned, but if I told you about them I would have to kill you.

5.63 | Overview
Overview of main screens
and features.

5.64 | Promotional image

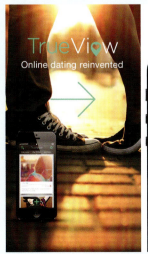

Workshop V:
It's all news to me

This workshop will help you get to grips with designing dynamic layouts that adjust for different screen sizes. This paper-based exercise is intended to take a couple of hours although it could be extended to a day if you wish to work up your ideas into more polished Photoshop visuals.

Background
The way we access news has changed radically in the last 20 years, from purchasing the morning newspaper and watching the evening television news to a 24/7 service where we can access news and information services from our smartphones.

The media formats for news are also merging; we expect to be able to access audio and video news articles as well as text-based services at the touch of button.

Furthermore, the source of our news providers is also changing as we can receive personalized news about our friends from their Facebook status updates or hear and see eye-witness accounts of breaking news stories from blogs, posts or tweets.

Brief
The objective of this workshop is to design an adaptive home-page layout for a local newspaper website. The layouts should be paper-based wireframes showing a series of viewport sizes.

The choice of newspaper is entirely up to you. A local newspaper is unlikely to have as sophisticated a web presence as a national news provider, so this is a real opportunity to investigate both the service they provide and its design layout.

The screen sizes required are:

1600x1200	browser
1024x768	browser, iPad (landscape)
800x480	Smartphone (landscape)
480x800	Smartphone (portrait)
320x240	feature phone

Step 1 – Research news
Look at the content of your chosen local newspaper. Assuming it has a website, make a careful note of its navigation, the number of news stories it features, advertising and other page information. Look carefully at each news story and note the different content elements, especially headline, image, byline, image, captions, etc.

Now look at a selection of national and international news services to see how they categorize and layout their home pages, and what other content and functions they provide; some examples are *bbc.co.uk*, *cnn.com*, *reuters.com*. You may also want to investigate a selection of rival local newspapers to see how their home pages differ.

Researching three to six alternative news providers would be more than sufficient for this exercise.

Step 2 – Content and functions
Make a list of the content and functions your home page should ideally include. Detail the number of stories and the story elements in particular.

Step 3 – Draw grids
Draw a set of rectangles that show the relative dimensions of the five viewports listed above.

Decide on the number of columns and important horizontal guidelines to create a modular grid and specify rectangular fields into which you can place content.

Step 4 – Navigation elements
Create thumbnail sketches based on your grid structure to start laying out essential global navigation elements. Be careful not to be over-generous with space for navigation elements, as the news stories will be the pages' features.

If you want to follow a 'progressive enhancement' approach, start with the mobile layout first, which will have the least available screen space, and then layer up additional navigation elements or features with each progressive screen size.

Don't be afraid to make numerous attempts for each screen size, as it is very unlikely that you will succeed at your first attempt.

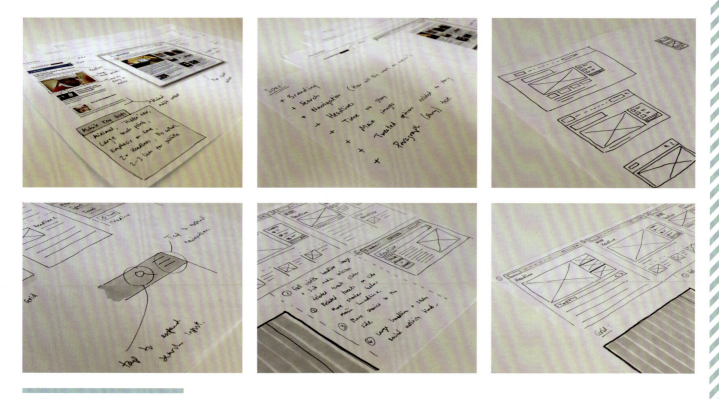

5.65–5.70 | The six steps
These layouts, created by David Ingledow, represent the six steps of the exercise: initial research, listing content and functions, drawing grids, navigation elements, adding content and creating final visuals.

Step 5 – Adding content

Once you are satisfied with your navigation elements, begin to layout your content. If you haven't already looked at mobile layouts for news sites, do so now. You will notice how simple some of the layouts are, particularly for feature phones and lower-resolution smartphones.

Following the suggestion in the last step, start with mobile first and then layer up content and expand your design across more columns with each new screen size.

Remember, it is unlikely that you will fit all your screen content onto a home page without the need for the user to scroll, so you can extend your design below the height of the screen; however, make sure all essential content is above it!

Step 6 – Final visuals

Once you have created a series of successful thumbnails for each screen size, it is time to work them up into more polished wireframe sketches.

Share your ideas with others if you have the opportunity to receive feedback and ideas on how to improve them.

Optional further steps

You may wish to take your design further by creating your wireframe on a computer using Adobe Illustrator or a more specialist wireframe package, such as Axure or HotGloo. This has the benefit of specifying in more detail the size of navigation elements, images and text.

You may even want to go one step beyond this and visualize final screen graphics in Adobe Photoshop or Illustrator.

Interactive design is a continually evolving field of creativity, which develops at the relentless pace of technological innovation. Therefore, when trying to explain the various forms of digital or interactive design, it is only possible to give a brief snapshot of the current state of the art.

The word 'format' by definition suggests that the design for each use is laid out or produced in a specific way. To some extent, this is true as there are of course various design components and requirements needed for different interactive formats such as web, mobile, games or television. However, the continual integration of the online world with television means that some of these formats, user interface patterns and the established design conventions behind them are beginning to blur, therefore creating new challenges and exciting opportunities for interactive design.

This chapter will highlight some of the tangible design assets or 'collateral' required by the different formats, but perhaps more importantly will explain some of the established design conventions or principles that underpin them.

Interactive formats

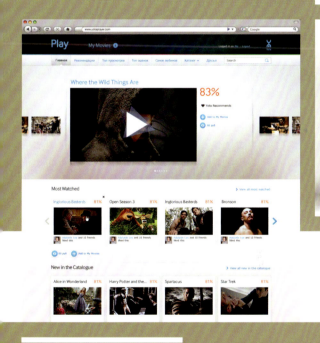

6

**6.01–6.03 | Combining social media
with on-demand services**
Yota Play was designed and developed
by All of Us: an interactive film and
television service in Russia. It is designed
for use over a 4G Internet network and
delivers a cross-platform experience
that combines social media with
on-demand services.

Web publishing

Unlike designing for print, or to a certain extent television graphics, web designers are rarely responsible for the individual layout of every published page. Most commercial websites are template-driven with pages dynamically created and served at the user's request. Designers are, of course, responsible for the design of templates and the graphical assets that are used within them.

Designing responsible and adaptive websites often means creating numerous versions of logos, buttons, banners and images that can work with various browser window sizes or viewports.

Designers who work closely with developers often create element sheets to communicate and share information about layout dimensions, typographic specifications and image use. These element sheets are then used to create the website's page designs and templates.

6.04–6.06 | Get Into Newcastle
The Get Into Newcastle website, designed by Komodo Digital, promotes the city centre of Newcastle upon Tyne and the huge range of businesses, venues, offers and events available to local residents and visitors. The site has dedicated desktop and mobile versions, helping users to pre-plan visits and access information and offers while on the move.

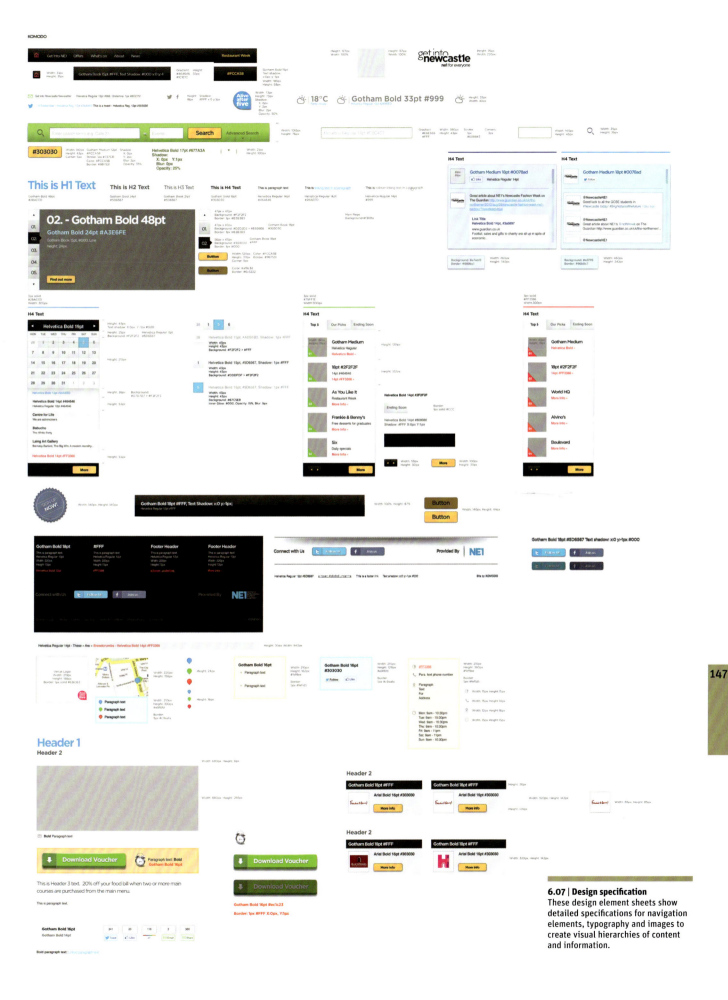

6.07 | Design specification
These design element sheets show detailed specifications for navigation elements, typography and images to create visual hierarchies of content and information.

An enhanced web experience

6.08–6.15 | *3 Dreams of Black*
3 Dreams of Black is an interactive film by Chris Milk, made with friends from Google. The film is a music promo for an album by Danger Mouse and Daniele Luppi, which features an immersive three-dimensional environment over which the user has some control. This creative and technological experiment showcases HTML5's canvas element.

An enhanced web experience → Online advertising and banner formats

Rich media enhancements

HTML5, CSS3 and web fonts are not only providing users with more aesthetically pleasing browsing, they are also leading to revolutionary new experiences. Users are now beginning to see greater use of immersive full-motion video and playful interaction. Still in its infancy, this technology is being used to create enhanced brand experiences rather than replace more established and practical forms of interaction, such as information-based searching and e-commerce transactions.

It will be interesting to see how businesses that rely heavily on design and strong visual messages – such as fashion, lifestyle and luxury brands – integrate the power of HTML5 with their often well-developed online shopping services to create websites that are both seductive and aspirational, yet efficient and practical.

6.16–6.20 | HTML5 canvas element
Blacknegative is a creative collective of directors, designers, developers and photographers whose portfolio website also uses the HTML5 canvas element, and supports audio and video to showcase stunning video clips that the user can seamlessly interact with.

149

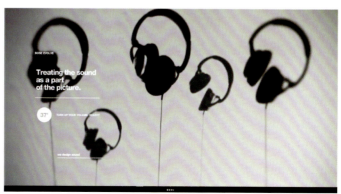

Online advertising and banner formats

Although, at times, it may seem that anything goes when it comes to online advertising, there are guidelines on the dimensions of ads and their file sizes. Standardizing the size of ads helps web publishers design advertising-friendly page layouts, and for ad agencies it means their ads will work across a range of potential advertising spots.

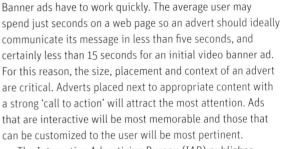

Banner ads have to work quickly. The average user may spend just seconds on a web page so an advert should ideally communicate its message in less than five seconds, and certainly less than 15 seconds for an initial video banner ad. For this reason, the size, placement and context of an advert are critical. Adverts placed next to appropriate content with a strong 'call to action' will attract the most attention. Ads that are interactive will be most memorable and those that can be customized to the user will be most pertinent.

The Interactive Advertising Bureau (IAB) publishes widely accepted guidelines on the dimensions, file sizes and interaction of online adverts. The guidelines are very thorough and stipulate the maximum lengths for video adverts, use of sound and maximum file size of adverts that have not been user-initiated. File size is very important, since users pay for data usage, particularly on mobile devices. Therefore, the IAB differentiates between 'polite' and 'user-initiated' file sizes so that users do not download large amounts of unwanted data.

The 'Mobile Rising Stars' diagram shows the latest web banner ad formats and dimensions known as 'units', which reflect both advances in technology and the popularity of formats. 'Mobile Rising Stars Ad Units' are a recent addition to the format guidelines and supplement the longer established Universal Ad Package (UAP) units with additional guidance on rich media elements such as pop-ups, floating adverts and interstitials (adverts between web pages).

6.21–6.25 | Axion banner concerts
This clever campaign for the Belgian youth band Axion, created by Boondoggle, organized a talent contest for 25 young up-and-coming bands. The bands were filmed and streamed in the frame of traditional banners. A voting system was installed for the public to elect a winner who won a real gig at Ancienne Belgique, one of Belgium's biggest concert halls.

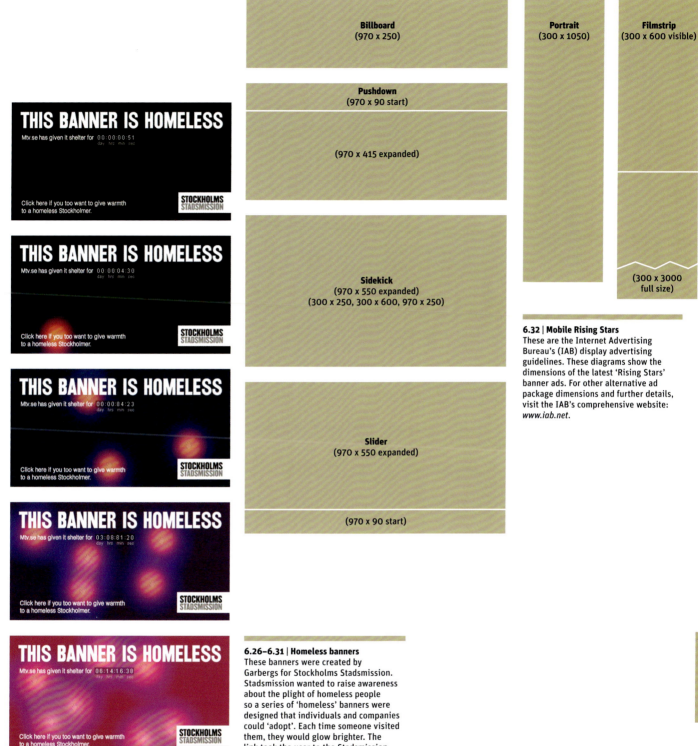

Billboard
(970 x 250)

Pushdown
(970 x 90 start)

(970 x 415 expanded)

Sidekick
(970 x 550 expanded)
(300 x 250, 300 x 600, 970 x 250)

Slider
(970 x 550 expanded)

(970 x 90 start)

Portrait
(300 x 1050)

Filmstrip
(300 x 600 visible)

(300 x 3000
full size)

6.32 | Mobile Rising Stars
These are the Internet Advertising Bureau's (IAB) display advertising guidelines. These diagrams show the dimensions of the latest 'Rising Stars' banner ads. For other alternative ad package dimensions and further details, visit the IAB's comprehensive website: *www.iab.net*.

6.26–6.31 | Homeless banners
These banners were created by Garbergs for Stockholms Stadsmission. Stadsmission wanted to raise awareness about the plight of homeless people so a series of 'homeless' banners were designed that individuals and companies could 'adopt'. Each time someone visited them, they would glow brighter. The link took the user to the Stadsmission website where they were invited to make a donation.

Mobile and tablet

6.33–6.34 |
Namedropper app
Developed by Komodo Digital, the app allows nightclub-goers to plan a VIP night out by adding their name to guest lists and rating their nights out. In return, night club event organizers build valuable mailing lists of club goers and their door staff use the app to check people in and out on their guest lists.

Back in 2006, Tomi Ahonen, the high-profile telecommunications consultant and author, stated that mobile was the 'seventh of the mass media'. He went on to explain that mobile was different from all its predecessors because it was personal, always on, carried by the user, had its own built-in payment system and was at the fingertips of creative inspiration. Smartphones have become ubiquitous, with their annual sales surpassing those for personal computers in 2011: a trend that many analysts claim will never be reversed.

For these reasons, the design of content for mobile devices has become a key area of growth and importance for interactive design. The implication for design layout is that an adaptive design approach that places mobile at the heart of internet-based communication is the way forward. However, there are more considerations for the design of successful mobile products than screen size and technology. According to Brian Fling in his excellent book *Mobile Design and Development*, context is everything for mobile design; knowing who your users are and what goal they are trying to achieve is key to creating a successful mobile website or app:

— Who are your users?
— What they are doing?
— What will they need?
— When will they use your app?
— Where are they?
— How will they use it?

There are many kinds of applications from information- and location-based services, such as news and maps, to productivity tools, such as email and games. Many services can be accessed through mobile sites or installed as native apps and games. By asking the questions listed you will understand your intended user's context much better, helping you make more informed decisions about what you design for them and how you implement it.

Practical advice for mobile design layout

There are a number of important considerations when designing for mobile:

— How will customers hold their device?
— Are they using a smartphone?
— How will mobile affect the design layout?

Mobile users tend to hold their device vertically in their non-dominant hand leaving their favoured hand for interaction. However, if they are playing a game, the tendency is to hold the mobile horizontally in both hands, leaving their thumbs free for interaction. Such concerns will all affect the placement of content and the method of interaction and gesture.

While touch-screen smartphones have overtaken the use of feature phones in many countries, it's still important to cater for users of feature phones with their use of the direction pad (D-pad) to access phone features, games and internet browsing. Whether designing for feature or smartphone, it is important to remember the mouse and cursor-based navigation experience, and user standard UX patterns to accommodate touch screen and directional pad input.

To help the user access content quickly, important content should be placed at the top of the screen with content getting more specific and in-depth the further a page is scrolled down. Lists of content or options should be stacked vertically as this is the natural scrolling direction.

For reasons of importance, many apps place their primary global navigation or most frequently used features in a fixed toolbar at the bottom of the screen within easy thumb reach.

Although smartphones are high resolution, their screens are tiny so care needs to be taken to make sure clickable areas are big enough for large fingers to operate. 44 x 44 points is the minimum acceptable size suggested by Apple for app development in their iOS Human Interface Guidelines.

Use vector graphics wherever possible, as they are scalable. In this vein, consider making icons into a custom-made font rather than individual bitmapped graphics so they will be rendered as vectors.

Finally, think about the situation in which the mobile is being used – if someone is walking around in the sun trying to use your new gardening and plants tips app, make sure the text is clear enough and you do not cram too much on one screen.

Keep your layout simple and reduce unnecessary features; for example, scroll bars are only necessary for visualizing your position within a block of content, so that you can make them much narrower.

6.35 | Guestlist
Facebook is a key component to the service; to access the full guest list functionality, users must sign in via their Facebook login, which in turn returns their list of friends. From here, they can create their own guest lists to as many nights as they 'like'.

6.36 | Event staff app
The guest list can be accessed through the 'event staff app' by door staff, allowing them to check guests in so that the system can measure who is attending and how many guests they are bringing – all in real time.

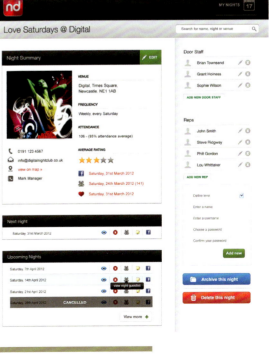

6.37 | Web admin panel
The event organizers can add and amend VIP nights and analyse guest list attendance and night ratings.

Games

Games design layouts differ from many of the examples previously discussed because the designs change dynamically with user interaction and often incorporate three-dimensional and motion-based elements. Therefore, the following sections concentrate on showcasing games aimed at different audiences with relevant theory and concepts to explain their game strategy and interface elements.

Children's games

When designing games or applications for pre-school children, there are three basic considerations: literacy, affordance and experience. If interaction or navigation is unclear, children have a tendency to click or touch everything in order to provoke a response, so providing obvious visual and audible cues is critical. It is also important to remember that a child's interactive experience is often limited to printed books, so simple page-based navigation is a solid metaphor to use.

Skoodle is an image manipulation iPad app developed by Plump Digital that tackles these issues successfully. The icon-based user-interface also makes good use of standard multi-touch UX patterns to paint, scale and twist stickers, which are intuitive for young minds with little fingers!

In contrast to *Skoodle*, *The End* for Channel 4 uses highly sophisticated gameplay in order to challenge adolescents' views about death, belief and science. The popular use of game dynamics to increase participation in non-game related subject matter is known as Gamification. *The End* encourages teenagers to explore the three game worlds of *Mind*, *Body* and *Spirit* to reveal their attitudes towards mortality. Players battle each world's guardians through strategic gameplay, puzzles and thought-provoking questions on a quest to collect prized Death Objects. These views are presented alongside those of their friends, as well as those of some of the most important thinkers of our time, including Gandhi, Descartes and Einstein.

6.38–6.42 | *Skoodle*
This iPad app enables children to take pictures or select an image to manipulate in four easy steps: select a photo, add stickers, paint and save. To keep interaction simple, icon-driven navigation is positioned at the bottom with a clear right arrow motioning progress to the next stage.

6.43 – 6.44 | *The End*

A free online educational game
designed and developed by Preloaded
for Channel 4's website. It is a game
of self-discovery for 14–19 year olds,
which integrates strategy, puzzles and
philosophical questions into a world that
explores a range of commonly (or less
commonly) held views about death, belief
and science.

6.45 | Dead Space 3
Developed by Visceral Games, this is an example of a diegetic user interface, where the action is seen from the game character's perspective. Even the game menu system is integrated into this view through access to in-game computer terminals. You can even 'mod' guns and share them with friends using the 'weapon bench'.

6.46 | HUD interfaces
Futuristic games often make use of augmented reality or heads-up-display (HUD) interfaces to give status information – this screenshot shows bullet count.

6.47–6.48 | Status indicators
The glowing backpack is also a status indicator; in the first case, it is used as an energy bar.

Games → Dual screens

Immersive games

Designing user experiences and interfaces reaches another level of complexity when creating three-dimensional worlds. Providing the user with intuitive game play and feedback on their interaction within their environment can be extremely challenging. *Mirror's Edge* is a first-person action-adventure platform game developed by EA Digital Illusions Creative Entertainment (DICE) in 2007, in which the player can move around a city environment running and jumping between buildings. In early user testing, the game was criticized for having unclear affordances and very difficult jumps. To resolve this, unreachable surfaces and buildings were moved further away, and objects that the player could interact with were coloured red. While this last feature could be viewed as unrealistic, the exaggerated use of colour was explained as 'runner vision', to give it credibility.

Creating a plausible premise for the presence of graphic user interface (UI) elements is integral to game narratives that place a premium on realism. Games that integrate UI elements within the game world are said to be 'diegetic' and those that have the UI placed outside or on top of the game world are 'non-diegetic'. In games that are set in the future, diegetic UI elements, such as game status information, are easier to explain by incorporating them as augmented or 'head-up-display' (HUD) interfaces.

The *Dead Space* series of sci-fi horror games is a prime example; game menus are accessed through computer terminals within the game world. The realism and horror is further enhanced by the removal of the ability to pause the game.

6.49–6.52 | *Mirror's Edge*
Created by EA Digital Illusions Creative Entertainment (DICE) and inspired by the free-running urban obstacle course discipline, 'parkour', *Mirror's Edge* is an innovative action-adventure game set in a dystopian world. The game interface helps the player see what objects can be interacted with by colouring them red, which it calls 'runner vision'.

6.53–6.56 | *Anthill*
Developed by Image & Form, this is a strategy game with an intuitive interface based on the real-world behaviour of ants. By drawing pheromone trails, the player directs their ground forces to different destinations, working with streams of units rather than individuals. The game incrementally builds players' knowledge and skills before putting their strategic ability to the test. Each mission is also time-limited, which is ideal for a casual game.

Casual games

In contrast to the high-premium shrink-wrapped box games, 'casual games' is a loose term used to describe a plethora of online games and downloadable phone app games that have simple rules and require little commitment to play. They typically appeal to an older and often female demographic.

For these reasons, the user experience and user interface need careful consideration to appeal to this less traditional games market. The game must have clear goals and rules. User interface needs to have instant visceral appeal and be easy to learn and play. Touch-screen controls for smartphones and tablets will require much simpler controls than a PC or dedicated games console.

The game play must have a strong intrinsic motivation to play with challenges that match the skill level of the player. This is an important aspect of designing successful user experience and interaction, and is based on the psychological concept of **flow**.

External games communities may provide further incentive to continue playing – for example, leader boards are a motivation for casual gamers, but multiplayer games are less popular because they are perceived as more demanding, less casual and time sensitive in nature.

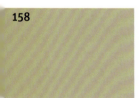

158

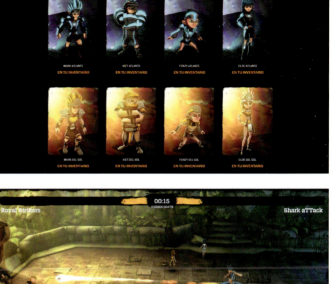

Games user interface tips

Good games user interfaces should:

1. Do what the player expects it to do.
2. Provide positive confirmation of player actions.
3. Provide relevant and timely information to the player.
4. Avoid clutter – no unnecessary or obtrusive UI elements.
5. Only be visible when necessary.
6. Icons should have a clear association with what they represent.
7. Use common conventions for status icons, such as hearts for health.
8. Adapt or evolve with game play.
9. Avoid placing UI elements in screen areas hidden by player's fingers and thumbs.
10. Be mindful that touch-screen inputs are not precise and need large active areas.

6.57–6.60 | *Desafío Champions*
Developed by Kotoc and TVE, *Desafío Champions* is an online game where two players face each other in a battle of fantasy football. The player controls four characters with unique characteristics and skills. Easy to learn but difficult to master, it appeals to both casual and hard-core players. The game is updated each week with new features, content and competitions.

Dual screens

Dual-screen viewing, where users browse the Internet or use social media while watching television, is becoming an increasingly popular social phenomenon; so much so that 75% of Americans who watch TV are dual screen viewing according to a study by Nielsen/Yahoo! People are not just keeping an eye on email or idly browsing, they are using services such as Zeebox in the UK, who provide related programme information, Twitter feeds and even chat with friends about the programmes they are simultaneously watching – a phenomenon known as 'back channelling'.

For design, the opportunities are not just information and social interaction based. The gamification of content and branded messages also provides users with engaging second screen experiences. AKQA's Star Player football app for Heineken encouraged fans of the UEFA Champion's League 2011/12 to compete with friends by asking them to make choices about what will happen next at key moments during a live match.

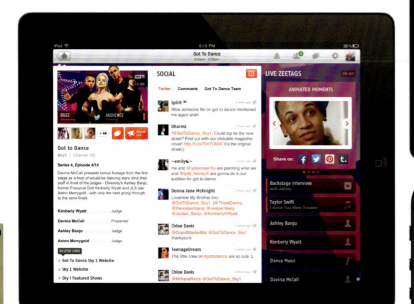

6.61–6.63 | Zeebox
A second screen guide to what's on TV and much more.

6.64–6.66 | Star Player
A football app for Heineken designed by AKQA, Star Player is a game that allows you to compete with friends by making correct decisions about what will happen next during a live UEFA Champion's League match.

TV graphics components

Television uses digital design in countless ways – from set design and animation through to continuity announcements and promotional literature. This section looks at how digital design is applied in a variety of uses.

Channel identities perhaps have to work harder than any design for a specific television programme, so looking at the range of on- and off-screen components will give a good grasp on how a design is used.

Components and terminology

Here are some common terms for television design components:

Break bumper is a short static or animated channel identity shown before or after a commercial break. Duration: 2–10 seconds.

DOG (*Digital On-screen Graphic*), or 'bug' in North America, refers to the logo watermark placed in the corner of broadcasts to reinforce a channel's identity and increase brand recognition.

End board or *End credit promotion* is a caption advertising another programme either at the end of a programme's credits or run side by side with the credits.

Ident is a short animation or video revealing the channel identity. Duration: 10–20 seconds.

Menu is an animated or still screen showing what is coming on now, next and later.

Sting is a short promotional advert for an individual programme, channel or season of programming. Duration: 10–30 seconds.

Title sequence is an animated or video-based introduction to a television programme or film revealing the title and main credits. Duration: 15 seconds or more.

6.67–6.70 | Syfy Channel
As rebranded by Proud Creative.
Top: 3D version of logo and still from 'carnival' ident.

Bottom: Still from 'liquid' ident and on-screen infographics.

162

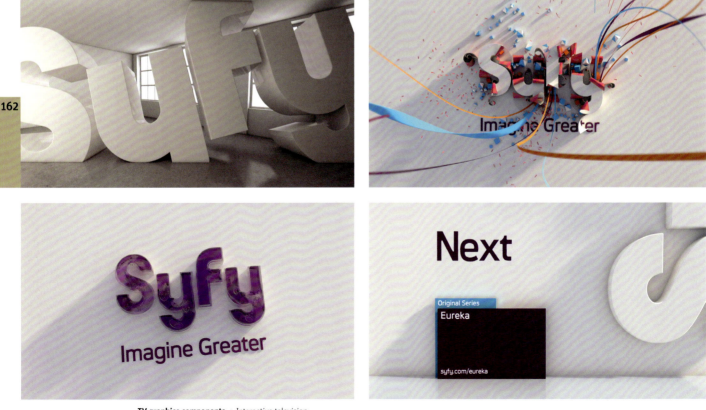

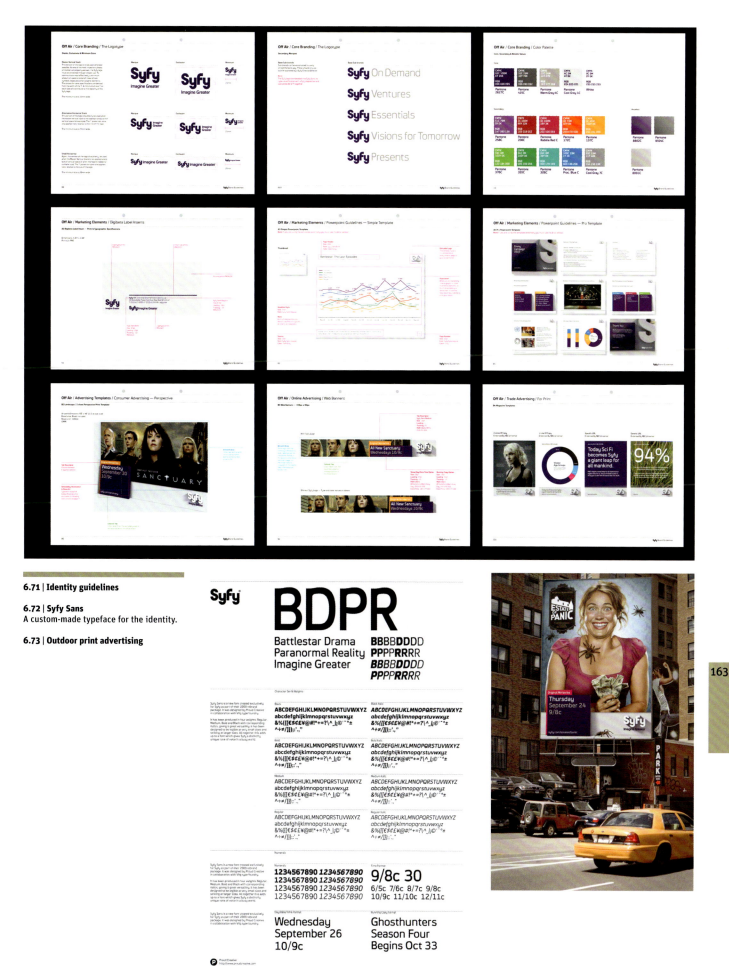

6.71 | Identity guidelines

6.72 | Syfy Sans
A custom-made typeface for the identity.

6.73 | Outdoor print advertising

Interactive television

Internet Protocol Television (IPTV) is a system through which services such as live TV, catch-up and video on demand (VOD) are delivered over the Internet. IPTV requires carefully considered user experience patterns – clarity and consistency are the keys to their successful design. There is no cursor on IPTV so the user navigates using the TV remote control with interactive elements highlighted by changes in colour or graphics. Each interactive element requires three button states to show the user what they can navigate and select: non-highlighted, highlighted, and highlighted and pressed.

To navigate interactive elements, the remote control's arrow keys and OK button are used as the primary means of navigation. The back button and coloured keys can also be programmed as quick links for navigation.

When designing IPTV content to support a live TV show, progressive revealing of information should be considered so that the viewer can continue watching while taking in additional information or selecting further options.

To access and display menu items or information, use familiar metaphors and idioms. Accordion panels and carousels are often used to display byte-size information and menu items, whereas pages, scrolling and tabs are commonly used to navigate screens with more information.

Occasionally, text fields or forms are required by the viewer for text input. Try to minimize their use, as using the TV remote control or an on-screen keyboard can be slow and tricky.

For more information on the design of television graphics, look at the BBC's Global Experience Language guidelines, where a lot of the advice above was drawn from *http://www.bbc.co.uk/gel/tv/device-considerations/designing-for-tv/introduction*.

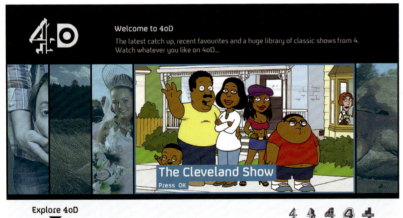

6.74–6.75 | IPTV interface
Channel 4's on-demand service (4oD) uses accordion and sliding panels to access content on its landing page. This IPTV interface was developed on the YouView platform in the UK by digital design studio, Ustwo.

6.76 | Smart Interaction features

The 4oD app for Samsung Smart TVs was released in 2013. Apps specifically built for Samsung's Smart TV range can take advantage of their Smart Interaction features, such as motion control, voice control and facial recognition.

6.77 | 4oD interface

A 4oD interface has been available for Sony PlayStation 3 since 2010. Services that are available on a number of different platforms, have the added challenge of balancing the consistency of service experience across platforms while working within established user interaction patterns and technical limitations for each device.

Formats without boundaries: Experiences and events

In contrast to on-screen interactions, there is also significant growth in experiential and event-driven communication. Experiential design is used to describe more physical interaction, such as interactive museum installations, that perhaps rely on input devices external to the computer, for example, pressure pads or cameras attached to microcontrollers.

Some experiences rely heavily on technology to create immersive experiences such as Nike+ FuelStation, which is a retail space featuring a seamless mix of innovative digital services and physical consumer experiences for 'digitally enabled athletes'.

With a similar approach to creative technology, Onedotzero and partners created an interactive installation to showcase six emerging DJs in the finale of Intel's PowerUp event at the Hoxton Gallery in London.

In contrast, other events use technology more invisibly to generate fervour and interest in a brand. Nissan's New Star of India short movie integrates social networking and a form of reality television to produce a unique branded event.

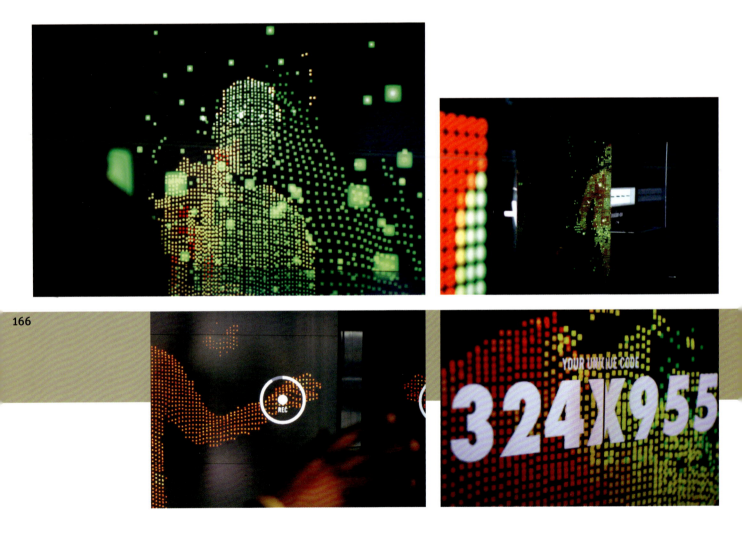

6.82–6.85 | New Star of India
AKQA created an innovative campaign that helped Nissan build a highly engaged community of nearly 500,000 fans on Facebook, and become one of the top automotive brands on Facebook in India. A talent hunt online gave Bollywood fans the opportunity of appearing in a movie with Ranbir Kapoor, one of Bollywood's hottest stars. They had to upload a short video clip of themselves dancing and encourage friends to vote for them on Facebook. Eventually, there were 20 lucky winners from all parts of India, selected by Ranbir and his team.

167

6.78–6.81 | Nike+ FuelStation
To bring the Nike+ FuelBand to life in-store, AKQA created Nike+ FuelStation, a motion-tracked installation where consumers can see a life-sized digitized reflection on an LCD wall that reacts to movement.

Interactive music installations
Not all interactive experiences are precision targeted for
an audience of one. Interactive music installations are
often a 'one to many' event as musicians, DJs and VJs
work with the audience to create both communal and
personal experiences.

6.86–6.93 | Intel PowerUp

For the finale of Intel's PowerUp with Ultrabook DJ competition, onedotzero teamed up with agency PD3 and Marshmallow Laser Feast to create a DJ-led interactive experience for a crowd of clubbers at the Hoxton Gallery in London.

The centrepiece was a '5D light reflection chamber' that was based around the concept of an infinity mirror to create an optical illusion. To create the fully immersive, audio-visual experience, a huge five-metre wall of controllable LEDs was used to create motion graphics. These visuals responded directly to the beat of the music and the gestures of the DJ.

Industry perspective: Charles Batho

Client
BBC

Brief
To design an educational game for the Children's BBC (CBBC) website on the theme of 'Create, Play and Share'.

Agency
Atticmedia

Solution
Game Builder is an Adobe Flash-based game that allows children to design and develop their own games and to share them with others.

6.94 | Charles Batho

Interview with Charles Batho, Creative Director
Charles has worked in creative direction and producer roles for a number of digital agencies and media companies, including Atticmedia, Preloaded and Time Warner. Charles specializes in games and engaging educational content.

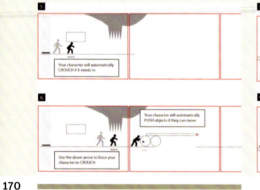

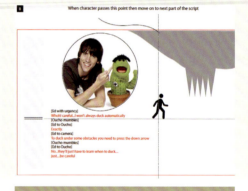

170

6.95–6.96 | Storyboards
Storyboards define player movement and interaction with 'enemies' from the outset.

6.97 | Tutorials
For the tutorial sections, a combined audio and visual script is required.

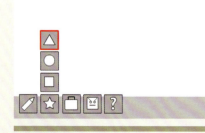

6.98 | Navigation
Early wireframes for the menu and tool navigation.

6.99 | Animation
Animation demos are generated to help refine character movements.

6.100 | Interactive characters
Interactive character demos are designed to test interaction with the game environment.

How did the project come about?

It was a self-initiated project in response to a call-out from the new BBC Vision commissioning system, who had asked for proposals on the theme of Create, Play and Share.

What form did the proposal take?

For the first stage, we simply submitted about seven or eight brief ideas in a written document. The BBC then came back to us asking for more detail about our 'Game Builder' concept.

How did you develop your proposal?

Initially, Game Builder was about being able to create your own narrative, adventure-style game. I felt this was too limiting and 'slow' for the intended audience. I wanted to do something much more arcade-like. In discussions around evolving the concept, we became aware of the 'Box 2D' physics engine, which had recently been ported to Flash. When I saw the demo, I knew that this was the engine we could build our game upon and the proposal coalesced around a platformer format. We resubmitted a more in-depth written proposal, outlining the core functions of the application, as well as a small Flash demo to illustrate the concepts.

Can you describe your development process?

Yes, it was an unusual process because normally we follow a standard development pathway where the project can be clearly scoped around a look and feel and a set of defined functionality that will be delivered. This was different because the technical foundation had to come first and the look of the project could then be fitted around that. I suppose it was a much more agile approach than we typically employ on Atticmedia projects.

How did it differ?

Essentially, we built a very small version of Game Builder as soon as we could and then added and refined the application in weekly iterations.

How did this affect your design process?

Well, as I said, normally you might start with the design and fit the functions to how you want the game to look. In the case of Game Builder, this was completely reversed. We had to define a set of characteristics and behaviours for gameplay rather than begin with a traditional storyboard of key frames.

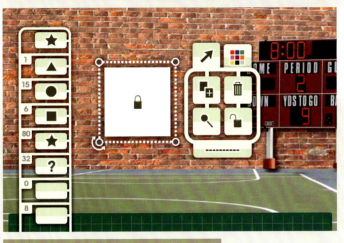

6.101 – 6.102 | Interactive demos
The functionality and learnability of the tools is assessed through interactive demos. A sample game level is created as quickly as possible to assess gameplay and technical development.

Industry perspective: Charles Batho

Were there any other difficult challenges for you to overcome?

One of the biggest was integrating with the BBC's back end infrastructure and working with tough moderation standards. Not only that, all the games and game assets needed to be held within a custom-made content management system (CMS) so that the BBC could update and maintain the games, as well as add or remove media assets. This was important so that the BBC could refresh content or moderate and remove user-created games.

Did this require a large team?

Surprisingly not. There were just two other full-time members of the team besides myself. I was responsible for the vision and shape of the overall project, including script, UX, music, etc. Nick Holliday created and led all the visual design and Lu Aye Oo was our lead Flash developer. One or two others helped shape the technical direction and development towards the start of the project, and we hired an animator and musician to help bring the project to life at the tail end of the project. We also worked with a couple of project managers and two developers from the BBC for the CMS development.

Did you have to do a lot of user testing?

Yes, we tested repeatedly with groups of school children. We did a great deal of research and testing to make sure that creating games was as easy as possible without limiting the user's creativity. We wanted creating a game to be as intuitive as picking up a set of pens and drawing on a piece of paper.

Did you learn anything important from the testing?

Yes, the language and pacing of how you teach 7–11 year olds is incredibly important. We also noticed subtle things when watching them play games, such as their fingers not being as nimble as you expect.

Testing is incredibly informative and will certainly improve the final product, but it's only useful if you are prepared to change the game and act on the feedback you get. It takes time and money to do it right, so you need to plan things carefully.

Are you pleased with the final result?

It's probably the one piece of work that I'm most proud of. It took much longer to develop than we ever envisaged due to various factors beyond our control, but the fact that it has been released is a testament to the commitment of all those involved. Almost 30,000 games have been created in the first four months, which is great.

Is that more than you anticipated?

Well, we worked on a 90:10:1 principle: 90% would play, 10% would rate other people's games and 1% would create their own, so if the principle holds true we've had a lot of games played in just the first four months!

6.103 | Game Builder main menu

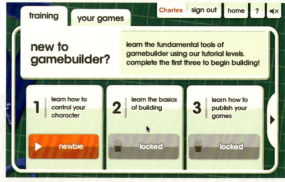

6.104 | Managing the challenges
The challenges are incrementally managed to build players' understanding and confidence.

6.105 | Choosing
The play menu allows the user to choose already created games.

6.106 | Game play kept simple
Left and right arrow keys are used to move your character and spacebar to jump.

6.107 | Facilitating learning
Players follow tutorials that use both visual and audio instructions to facilitate learning.

6.108 | Building and customizing
Object palettes for building and customizing your game resemble the aesthetic of an Airfix kit.

6.109 | Sharing
Players are encouraged to share their games with friends via email.

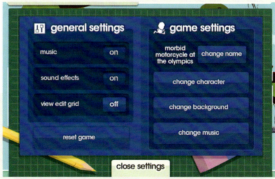

6.110 | Game Builder
A highly customizable and very sophisticated application, but the interface has to be kept as simple as possible for the audience age group.

Workshop VI:
One message, many formats

This workshop encourages you to laterally develop a digital campaign that works across a number of formats. The workshop is intended as a paper-and-pencil-based exercise with 60–120 minutes recommended for completion.

Background

Online advertising has grown in complexity as fast as the technology that has enabled it. From a standing start 20 years ago, digital campaigns have grown from simple banner ads to highly sophisticated campaigns that traverse both traditional and online media. The latter has become particularly attractive for advertisers, as it can be precision targeted towards its intended audience and has the additional benefit of being a relatively low-cost medium, particularly if a campaign goes 'viral'.

In 2010, Ashley Ringrose, founder of digital agency Soap Creative, gave a presentation at Advertising Age's digital conference, where he presented six foundations for successful digital campaigns, which he identified as: Interactive, Customizable, Contextual, Entertaining, Playable and Useful. These foundations will form the basis of this workshop.

Brief

Your brief is to design a digital campaign to sell one of the following products to a particularly challenging audience:

Coals to Newcastle
Coffee to Colombia
Owls to Athens
Sand to Arabs
Snow to Eskimos
Tea to China

These products and their intended audience are based on famous idioms or phrases. You may want to research their origins before beginning the task! The following steps will focus on Ashley Ringrose's six foundations in order to create a digital campaign.

Step 1 – Interactive

Select one of the idioms above as the basis for your campaign. Your first challenge is to design a banner ad. Your concept should encourage the user to click on the ad, as interactivity with a banner increases brand recall by over 60% according to Barnum Sulley Research (2010). You may choose either a horizontal or a vertical banner ad and draw simple sketches for your concept.

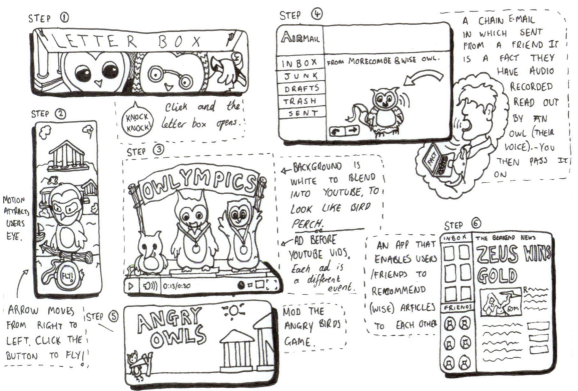

6.111 | Owls to Athens
These sketches by Max Holford illustrate concepts for the 'Owls to Athens' campaign formed from the six steps.

Step 2 – Customizable

Ads that encourage the user to customize them by entering data – their location, age, etc – or by moving sliders will increase the user's interest, particularly if there is a quick reward for their interaction. Draw another concept that tempts the user to customize the ad.

Step 3 – Contextual

Sometimes, the media placement of an ad is just as important as the creative concept. Ads that take full advantage of the context in which they are placed will also encourage user interaction. Think about the websites on which you would place your ad. Write them down. Design another ad that could be designed around the web page's content.

Step 4 – Entertaining

Moving away from banner ads, viral campaigns in the form of emails or text messages that are thought-provoking or entertaining will be remembered and shared. Try to think of the kinds of emails that you have received and found entertaining and then passed on to friends – were they jokes, hoaxes or links to amazing videos? What would work for your campaign? Sketch it out.

Step 5 – Playable

Imagine designing a game for your campaign. In 2011, Lady Gaga released 'Gagaville' on Facebook, a customized version of the popular casual game 'Farmville' to promote her new album. What game could you modify for your campaign? Draw some screenshots of your game to show how the game could be modified.

Step 6 – Useful

Some campaigns create useful services for their users that do not necessarily have any direct link with the product they are trying to sell. These campaigns tend to build affinity with a brand and customer loyalty rather than direct sales.

Think carefully about your audience. What would they most value? What would interest them? It may be a sport or leisure activity, or a culturally significant event or a festival. Imagine what service you could provide them in the form of an app or website.

175

The ability to create wonderful interactive projects can easily be undermined by ineffectual presentation or poor communication. It is not unusual for designers who confidently communicate a product or service's value through their design work to be more uncertain and withdrawn in a presentation situation. It is also easy to become complacent on completion of a demanding project and neglect to promote its value through a portfolio website. Yet, as designers, there is little excuse for these potential shortcomings as we have the intellectual understanding and practical skills required to present and communicate ideas effectively.

This final chapter focuses on the successful presentation of projects and the creation of portfolios to promote design work. The first half of this chapter will discuss the preparation, benefits and tools required to produce both digital and physical presentations. The second half will focus on the promotion and showcasing of design work. It will also mirror the first half by highlighting the advantages and requirements for the creation of both digital and physical portfolios.

Presenting your ideas

7.01–7.05 | Presentation

This chapter draws on work produced by both established design agencies and design students. Easy-to-use digital design tools and inexpensive online promotion are visually narrowing the gap between the skilled novice and the seasoned professional. However, experience is a huge differentiator when it comes to the verbal presentation of concepts and delivery of complex projects.

Preparing for a presentation

Whether you are an experienced designer or a design student, presenting work takes a great deal of preparation. Occasionally, great design work sells itself, but most of the time we have to exercise skill in presenting our design so that it is received in the way that we intended.

Fifteen years ago, presenting interactive work used to be pure theatre, with clients staring in wonder at what they might see, and the creative team holding their breath in case a technical demonstration did not work. These days, interactive design is no longer a dark art shrouded in mystery; clients usually have a clear understanding of what they are commissioning and have high expectations of what can be delivered. The medium has lost none of its magic, but we can no longer expect clients to become spellbound at the first sight of some clever interaction.

When preparing for a presentation, we continually need to ask ourselves the same fundamental questions: What is the purpose of the presentation? Who are we presenting to? What are their expectations? How can the presentation address those needs? Where will we be presenting? What tools will we use?

Presentation goals and content

The purpose, content and format of a presentation will be dictated by your relationship with the client and the phase in the development cycle of a project. For example, is it a credentials presentation for a prospective client or a concept presentation for an existing client?

Each presentation will have specific goals, so it is important to remain focused on achieving them. In preparation, write down the goals and decide how your presentation will demonstrate their accomplishment. Briefly explain upfront what you understand is the purpose of the presentation and what you will be sharing with them. This recap is particularly useful when presenting to a number of people from the client's organization, as not everyone may be up to speed with the current status of the project. It will also highlight any differences in expectation, which can be addressed, or at least understood, at the outset of the presentation.

It is well worth doing your homework on new clients creative expectations before undertaking design work. Clients often set briefs that ask for a 'creative', 'innovative' or 'fresh' solution, but these adjectives are highly subjective and can lead to potential misunderstandings. A quick review of the kinds of design work that a client has previously commissioned will tell you a lot about how conservative or adventurous they may be.

The content of your presentation should focus entirely on addressing the presentation goals – but how you present your work also needs careful scrutiny. In an early concept generation phase, it is often prudent not to produce overly polished visuals before the client has bought into an idea. Apart from labour saving, visuals that look finished can incite wrath rather than praise if the client sees flaws in something that looks complete, making the designer look careless or overconfident.

A presentation is not a one-way process solely for the client's benefit. If you are expected to formally present work through the different phases of the project, it is shrewd to make the format work hard for you by asking your clients to respond to questions and make decisions at these meetings. Your time, and the client's, is precious so it is important to make the most of these opportunities when all the decision-makers are likely to be in the room.

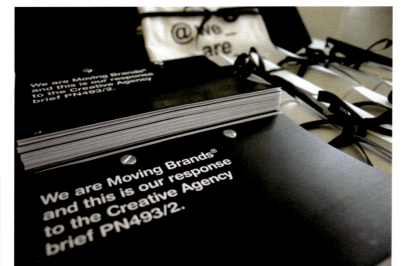

7.06 | 'Hero' pitch box
A Brand for London,
by Moving Brands.

We are Moving Brands®
and this is our response
to the Creative Agency
brief PN493/2.

Like you, we
believe that
this process
must engage
with people

So that's exactly what we've done. Fusing
public involvement with brand creation to
develop the Brand for London.

**It's going to be a living identity to take
us all to 2012 and beyond.**

We've created a home for ideas to be aired and shared
www.abrandforlondon.wordpress.com

All the thinking and
creation has been
posted here. Everything
invites comments and
participation. The creative
and intellectual story has
just begun to live in the
world.

**The debate has
begun.**

We have engaged the
Twitter community
in debate. We ask,
they tell, they ask, we
explain, we question,
they explain.
We all learn.

It's creating quite a stir...

Blog   **40,000+** visits
Twitter   **500+** followers
Media   **Evening Standard
The London Paper
Design Week**

And all in just 8 days - People want to be involved

**Why are we approaching the task
like this?**

Every brand needs a compelling story at its heart.

The story drives the expression: visual, tone of voice,
logo and experience across all touchpoints - print,
web, screen and face-to-face.

We've gone direct to London to get the input we
need to create the story.

All our creative work
to date is on the site
with all the feedback
and suggestions from
the people of London
(and around the world).
We are absorbing and
learning from what
people have to say. We
look forward to sharing
it with you face to face.

What's still missing from the mix?

– Your team's knowledge, experience and input.

– The learnings from your partners: Saffron,
Wolff Olins etc...

– The opportunity to collaborate and shape
the creative solution together.

– The feedback we will then seek from
London itself.

We've got a great team.

Swisscom – we modernised
a national treasure.

We've brought tradition
into the 21st century.

Obama – the most innovative political campaign ever

Working with Scott Thomas will bring a wealth of learning in
how social media captures the hearts and minds of a population,
passing power and ownership back to them.

What we will deliver:

A world-class Brand for London on November 1st,
designed by all of us, for use by all of us.

Created openly by professionals, influenced by those
who choose to talk to us.

**London never stands still, nor should
the brand or the team.**

**The Brand Story is out there
and rapidly gathering momentum.
Our insights are growing with it.**

**We can't wait to share our learning,
process, creative approach, insight
and designs with you next week.**

Come and visit our blog

40,000
other people already have

www.abrandforlondon.wordpress.com

Camilla Grey
Marketing Manager
camilla.grey@movingbrands.com

Moving Brands
7 & Charlotte Rd
London, EC2A 3DH

Phone 020 7739 7700
Fax 020 7739 7020
www.movingbrands.com

7.07–7.24 | A Brand for London

This is a daring and very public
presentation conceived by Moving Brands.
Moving Brands had already consulted
the entire world through an open blog
inviting contributions before attending
the actual pitch presentation. The blog
received 40,000 visits and had generated
stories in the national press.

Additional presentation advice

Presentations can be intimidating, particularly if presenting to large groups or new clients, so it is essential to draw confidence from your work, and never fall into the trap of making advanced apologies for what you are about to present. Designers have a tendency to see the shortcomings in their own work; self-criticism is both a professional virtue and flaw, so it is vital not to let self doubt surface under pressure. Be confident and defend your work. Accept constructive criticism gracefully, but do not draw attention to your own shortcomings voluntarily; it will neither help sell your concept nor will it make the client feel confident about their decision to hire you in the first place.

An experienced presenter will foresee any curveballs thrown up by an unfamiliar presentation room, projector or sound system that they will be required to use. Designers are generally happier to present work in their own studio meeting room where the environment is controlled and the technology is familiar; however, clients often prefer to have work presented at their own offices for convenience. In this circumstance, it is sensible to ask your client about the suitability of the designated room and what equipment will be available. Time permitting, you should visit the room in advance and test the equipment.

Above all, an experienced presenter will rehearse or run through an important presentation to make sure that what they say complements and emphasizes their digital presentation in order to communicate their points effectively and satisfy their audience.

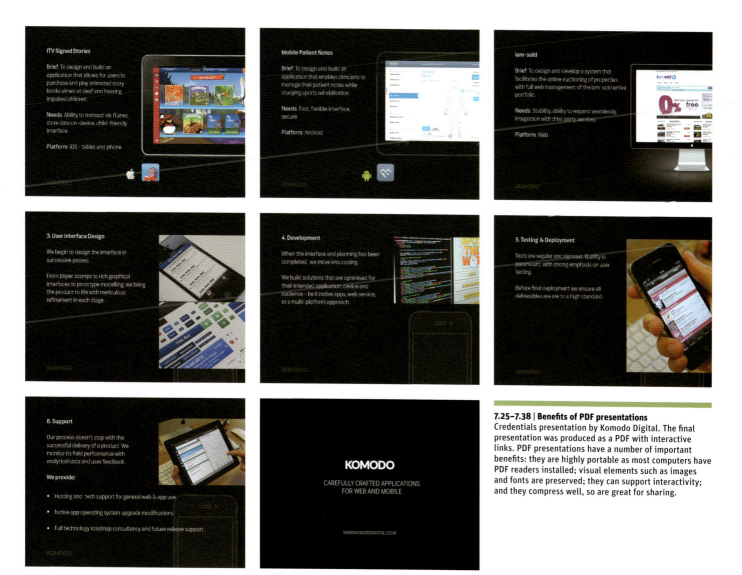

7.25–7.38 | Benefits of PDF presentations

Credentials presentation by Komodo Digital. The final presentation was produced as a PDF with interactive links. PDF presentations have a number of important benefits: they are highly portable as most computers have PDF readers installed; visual elements such as images and fonts are preserved; they can support interactivity; and they compress well, so are great for sharing.

Digital presentations

Digital presentations are by their very nature a standard method used to communicate interactive work. They have many obvious benefits, but they are not easy to get right; there is much more to them than sequencing a set of slides in Apple Keynote.

Digital presentations are highly portable, easy to edit and share. Their illuminated glow can be very seductive and naturally showcases interactive and audio-visual work well. For the self-conscious presenter, they helpfully focus the audience's attention on the screen rather than themselves.

Their downside is the default way in which digital presentations are used. Many of us have experienced 'death by PowerPoint', which often reflects a lack of preparation or consideration by the presenter rather than any inherent issue with the software. To avoid this happening, digital presentations should be succinct with engaging content that is carefully edited.

Digital presentations should have a consistency of visual language. Key points may be bulleted, but try to add a little visual interest by designing your own slide templates. However, do not over-design them, as this will detract from your presentation's content. Use clear visual breaks between sections of a presentation. Animated elements should be purposeful to emphasize points rather than bedazzle the audience. As with a brochure or magazine, a long presentation should establish a visual pace and rhythm, which helps to maintain interest and clarity of message.

A common mistake made by presenters is to read verbatim on-screen bullet points. By all means, emphasize important points by repeating them, but try to script your presentation so that your spoken delivery complements rather than duplicates on-screen content.

7.39–7.50 | Revel – a social food app
This is a student project by Ryan Coupe, Luke Emmerson and David Ingledow. This concept and early development presentation authored in Keynote explains their concept, visual research, identity development, initial paper prototyping and project timeline.

A social driven app that persuades users, through a benefit and reward scheme, to be creative with homemade lunches. This is to promote the reduction of food packaging.

To create an identity that has a personable approach conveyed through a clean and minimal interface that communicates effectively to a student and young professional audience.

182

Digital presentation tools

Apple Keynote and PowerPoint are commonly used presentation tools as they are relatively simple to use and can integrate images, movies and website links well. You can also make good use of their 'notes pane' in 'presenter view' to show your script or slide notes. Care needs to be taken when moving presentations between computers to make sure that they have compatible software and that external files, such as movies and fonts, are included. If you present your slideshow from a remote file space in the 'cloud', then a stable and fast Internet connection will be required. This will be essential if you are planning to use Internet-based tools, such as Projeqt or Prezi. The latter is particularly good for creating dynamic pseudo three-dimensional presentations.

Digital presentations will inevitably require the hands-on use of prototypes at some stage in the project's development cycle. These hands-on demonstrations will need careful management and choreographing if they are part of a formal presentation. If staged well, these participatory demos can add a lot to the impact and value of a presentation.

Digital presentations do not have to be exclusively technology based. Printed slides and notes are often made available for clients to read during the presentation, make notes on, and take away. The question of when to provide presentation notes requires a judgement call. Presentation notes shared beforehand may guarantee that your audience will not miss key points and will be less distracted by a need to take copious notes; however, it reduces anticipation and surprise, and may reduce attention if they are particularly detailed, in which case some agencies prefer to provide handouts at the end of a presentation.

When sharing digital presentations with clients or colleagues afterwards, it is often safer to share them using a PDF format to ensure that they work correctly and fonts are not substituted. For presentations that include audio and video elements, uploading them to a secure online file space is another alternative.

7.51–7.54 | Revel application presentation boards
Produced by Ryan Coupe, Luke Emmerson and David Ingledow, these four physical boards were accompanied by a two-minute promotional film and website explaining how the app worked, and a demo app on an iPhone authored in Proto.io for the audience to play with.

Physical presentations

Two of the most common gripes that designers share are: their client 'doesn't understand how much work goes into making their project...'; and their client 'won't pay for development work...'. These issues are not just felt by start-up design studios, but are also keenly felt by many established agencies. One presentation method that helps to address these issues (but won't necessarily solve them) is to present the story of your project development using a physical presentation format.

This does not mean mounting work on foam board, which may feel pretty pointless for interactive or digital work. It means to print out, sort, label and present research, early ideas generation and development work in a physical environment, usually a room with a large wall. The work is displayed in a horizontal chronological order so that the client can literally be walked and talked along the development path, visually seeing sketches, concepts and decision-making points that lead through to a final design proposal.

This process has many virtues for the designer and their client, as the designer's thinking, skills, and late-night hours of development can be laid bare for the client to see. Designers can learn directly where on the development path a positive or negative assumption or decision about the client's product or service was made. Clients live and breathe the creative process, and feel they are on a journey with the designer and their decision-making process.

It is rare to find a client who does not appreciate your work or the time and effort that you have put in after taking this physical presentation journey. They may not always agree with your creative decisions, but they will understand them better.

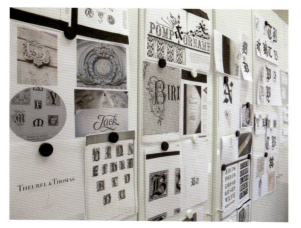

7.55–7.60 | Trend Bible rebrand

Trend Bible rebrand and visual identity system by Gardiner Richardson. Trend Bible, a trend-forecasting agency, wanted their identity to better reflect their growing maturity and sophistication while retaining their charm and personality. These images show how Gardiner Richardson physically presented the visual development of an identity to make a compelling argument. The final images show finished brand touchpoints, such as the logo, client folder and website.

Creating portfolios

Portfolios are the key promotional tools for designers. They showcase our experience and expertise, who we have worked for and often our working processes, too. Adrian Shaughnessy astutely points out in his seminal book, *How to be a Graphic Designer without Losing Your Soul*, that there is a subtle but important difference in the content of portfolios between individual designers and design studios. Designers' own portfolios tend to showcase skills and working methods in order to impress other designers and the studios that might employ them, whereas design studio or agency portfolios focus on demonstrating capabilities and credibility to prospective clients.

Designers working in digital and interactive platforms invariably use digital portfolios in the form of websites and presentations to share work with potential employers and clients. However, printed portfolios have their place, too, as they are great for showing detailed flows and sequences of layout and are resistant to occasional, but awkward, technology failure.

Digital portfolios

An online portfolio has many advantages for the designer and their prospective clients. For the designer, it is easily updateable, always available and easy to share. They are clearly great for showing interactive and time-based work, and in comparison with physical portfolios, they are easy to carry and hard to lose! For prospective clients, they are convenient, usually informative and give the viewer anonymity so that they can look at a designer's work without being pestered by follow-up telephone calls or emails.

What should a website include?

Sections on who you are and what you do are important; these should explain your values and working methods as a design practitioner, and may help differentiate you from your competition.

A portfolio section on your work is essential, and the work should demonstrate your expertise and experience. For experienced designers and studios, a client list is also recommended as this gives prospective clients confidence that you have successfully completed project work. Client lists and client testimonials are a form of external validation; if you say you have a certain level of expertise and clients are happy to recommend you, then it stands to reason that you are most likely competent and trustworthy.

The website should also include essential contact information and a contact form allowing you to collect important details about the nature of an enquiry and the prospective client, too. Remember, clients rarely give their business on the strength of your website alone; however, it can make them confident that they have found the right designer or agency with whom they can begin a discussion about prospective work.

How should project work be organized?

Each project should begin with an explanatory text covering the problem set, your solution and the results of your design work. Write a concise overview of the client's initial problem, challenge or opportunity; this may take the form of a summary of the client's brief. This should be followed by a short description of your solution, detailing what you did, how you did it and why. The results demonstrate how effective your design was in meeting the client's needs – it may have increased sales, awareness of a client's services or the improved performance of a product, for example, a client's website.

edenspiekermann_
projects

edenspiekermann_
volkswagen

service design design thinking automotive interaction design iphone app innovation prototyping app
user experience mobile experiences   Robert Stulle

edenspiekermann_
about

Trust us. You hired us because we can do something you cannot do.   ⊕

We design brand experiences. We start with a strategy, choose the appropriate media to deliver it and then design the complete experience.

Wir gestalten Markenerlebnisse. Wir beginnen mit der Strategie, wählen die angemessenen Medien und gestalten dann das komplette Erlebnis.

Wij ontwerpen merkbeleving. We beginnen met strategie, kiezen de juiste communicatiekanalen en ontwerpen dan de complete ervaring.

What we do

Clients have remarked that we have an attitude. We take that as a compliment. Read our manifesto and you'll see why. This attitude doesn't attract every client under the sun, but we have built some strong and long-lasting relationships with those clients who appreciate our dedication and our beliefs. A few of those beliefs may help you to understand where we're coming from and where we may take you:

Good ideas have no sell-by date. Trends change,

Auftraggeber sagen uns eine gewisse Haltung nach. Das nehmen wir als Kompliment. Wenn Sie unser Manifest lesen, wissen Sie, warum. Diese Einstellung mag nicht zu jedem Auftraggeber passen, aber wir haben im Laufe der Zeit starke und lange währende Beziehungen zu denen aufgebaut, die unsere Hingabe schätzen und unsere Ansichten teilen. Ein paar Sätze mögen helfen zu verstehen, woher wir kommen und wohin der gemeinsame Weg uns führen könnte:

Klanten vinden dat wij een bepaalde 'attitude' hebben. Wij vinden dat een compliment. Lees ons manifesto en u zult begrijpen waarom. Deze houding spreekt niet elke klant aan, maar we hebben een sterke relatie opgebouwd met klanten die onze toewijding en onze overtuigingen waarderen. Een aantal van deze overtuigingen geven aan waar we vandaan komen en waar wij u naar toe kunnen leiden:

---

edenspiekermann_
blog

ESPI on stage: Harry Keller at Creative Mornings

Harry Keller was the first of us to rush onto the stage of Creative Mornings Berlin at Orangelab (many of us in the audience, of course). His issue: How our roles as designers and coders (and project managers, and ...) are changing and will – should! – change further in the near future. As a case he referred to the website we designed for Ableton, which became one of the top 25 responsive sites of 2012. We started with HTML prototypes right away (not static mock-ups). Harry described our iterative team work and how this can be much more efficient than traditional ways of working for clients.

 Sonja Knecht

December 20, 2012 13:50

people service design espi-on-site harry keller responsive web design

To be continued in 2013.   Even changes change all the time.

After welcoming the audience "to the era of excellence", Harry explained traditional workflows as being "often too waterfallish" and summed up the advantages of iterative processes: "The result is probably not what you expected, but exactly what you need" – „immediate stakeholder feedback" being one decisive thing.

„Asking is a strength."   exactly the result you need.

👍 Like 5 🔗 ✈ Tweet 0

No Risk, No Scrum

Johannes Cordes

December 17, 2012 14:05

iterative process scrum project management agile webdesign agile process

Agiler, schlanker, offener, durchlässiger, spielerischer ... kurz: einfach besser. Im Oktober habe ich endlich meine Schulung zum Scrum-Master machen dürfen und bin damit jetzt einer der „Wissenden". Ich kannte Scrum als Begriff bis dahin nur aus der Software-Entwicklung. Und so fand ich mich in der Schulung auch inmitten von Programmierern, Developern und IT-Beratern wieder: als klassischer Accountmanager mit „analogem" Background eine Art Paradiesvogel? Nein, denn wir wissen längst, dass Scrum sich letztlich bei all unseren Projekten (Markenentwicklung, Service Design, Corporate Identity, Corporate Design) anwenden lässt – sofern unsere Auftraggeber mitspielen.

Als Testszenario im Workshop ...   ... Stadtentwicklung via Scrum

Jenseits der Online-Offline-Debatte: Die reine Lehre beschreibt Scrum als Methode, um komplexe Produktentwicklungen in einem interdisziplinären Team möglichst schnell, kostengünstig und

---

7.61–7.65 | Qualities of a website
Edenspiekermann is a strategic brand experience design agency and their portfolio website imbues their qualities and values with confidence. The website content is engaging and informative, and its design features beautifully crafted layouts with an elegant use of web fonts.

7.66–7.68 | Graduate's personal website by Husam Elfaki

This attractive website features in-depth explanations of Husam's personal and collaborative work, demonstrating his working process as well as his final outcomes. Like agency websites, Husam features the logos of companies he has worked for and student competition brief sponsors as a form of external validation.

Creating portfolios → Industry perspective

Creating online portfolios

Portfolio websites are a labour of love for most designers, and the time they take to produce will largely depend on the complexity of your design and your personal motivation to learn new web skills. Portfolio sites generally fall into three categories: custom-made, template-based and communal.

Custom-made websites are hand-coded websites usually written in HTML5 and CSS3, or authored using a WSIWYG editor such as Adobe Dreamweaver. The benefit of this approach is that you can make your website exactly how you want it to function and look; the downside is that they can take considerable time to develop and, depending on your level of technical expertise, updating them can also be time consuming.

Template-based sites use existing templates or content management systems (CMS) to create websites quickly. These template-based systems can be customized to give the designer control over how they visually appear. These systems often incorporate blog features and easy-to-use interfaces for the management of content. Popular template-driven content management systems used by designers include WordPress, Drupal, Blogger and Cargo Collective. The benefits of these systems are their simplicity of use and how they incorporate complex functionality with relative ease. Their only slight drawback is that, if you are striving for a unique layout and aesthetic with custom-made functionality, it may be easier to write your own code rather than adapt an existing template.

For designers not wishing to create their own websites, an alternative is to post work and contact information on design related communal websites, such as Behance, Carbonmade, design:related or Dribbble. These design community sites give designers the opportunity to upload and share their work, make contacts and find employment. For these reasons, portfolio work placed on communal websites is viewed as a supplementary promotional activity to the creation of personal websites.

Design community websites and their benefits

Authoring tools	Template-based websites	Communal websites
Adobe Dreamweaver	blogger.com	behance.net
Coda 2 – Panic	cargocollective.com	carbonmade.com
CoffeeCup HTML Editor	drupal.org	designrelated.com
Komodo Edit	indexhibit.org	deviantart.com
Microsoft Expression Web	joomla.co.uk	dribbble.com
Notepad++	vbulletin.com	flickr.com
TextEdit	wordpress.org	hunie.co

7.69–7.74 | Organization and thinking skills

Portfolio spreads from Lukas Schrank's graduate portfolio. The spreads not only showcase Lukas's design and drawing skills, but his organization and thinking skills too, through their layout and project explanations.

Lukas Schrank Portfolio

Creating portfolios → Industry perspective

Analogue portfolios

Printed portfolios are naturally great for showing print-based work where the choice of materials and finish are paramount. They are also extremely robust as they do not rely on technology to view them, making them impervious to computer hardware or software failure, lack of power or Internet connection and overly bright lighting conditions! For these reasons alone, it is always advisable to create a paper-based portfolio as a backup. A4 is a handy size, but A3 is better as spreads are large enough to create impact and to display a number of images on a single page.

Printed portfolios are generally presented in person; however, designers looking for work are often asked to leave their folios for art directors to view at their convenience. In either case, the portfolio needs to speak for you. Work should be clearly and consistently labelled and explained, and projects chosen for inclusion should be relevant to the client or studio that you are visiting.

Physical portfolio tips

1 A3 is the most versatile size (11.7x16.5 inches).

2 Mount your work on thin card and avoid window mounting.

3 Select the most relevant work for your prospective client or employer.

4 Three to six projects is usually enough.

5 Order projects with a good start, middle and end.

6 Use a simple consistent grid layout and do not over-clutter.

7 Take good photos of important 3D objects, paper prototypes, etc.

8 Include short explanations of your project brief, solution and results, if known.

9 Show examples of work in context, such as websites on monitors or apps on smartphones, etc.

10 Create impact by using the double-page format effectively.

11 Good portfolios create a natural viewing 'rhythm'.

12 Remember narrative: you're telling the story of the projects and your expertise and experience!

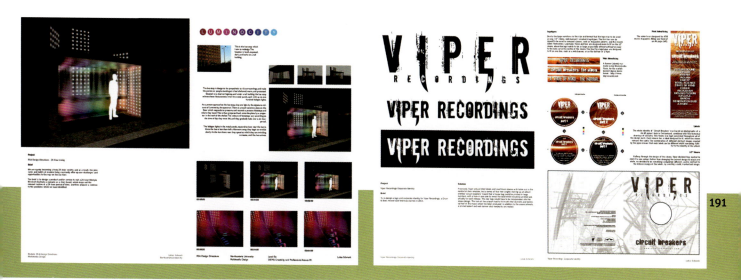

7.75–7.76 | Retaining a project's individuality
These are printed portfolio sleeves by Lukas Schrank. The spreads have a natural order and rhythm, yet each project retains its individuality.

Industry perspective:
William Lidstone, Razorfish

Agency
Razorfish

Project
Storytelling workshop and presentation slide deck
for Razorfish staff to improve their pitch and
presentation planning.

7.77 | William Lidstone

**Interview with William Lidstone, Executive Vice President,
Razorfish International**
William has worked in leading digital agencies, such as
Razorfish and AKQA, for almost 20 years, where he has
worked primarily in client services and planning roles
on awarding-winning digital work for numerous
international brands.

7.78–7.79 | Storytelling
These graphics were created by Razorfish to illustrate
William Lidstone's 'storytelling workshop', which is
designed to help Razorfish employees pitch ideas with
a greater degree of professionalism and success.

What made you decide to create the storytelling deck?
I've found over the years by making lots and lots of mistakes that there are good ways and bad ways of presenting work. If you stick to certain basic rules, things work smoothly and if you break some of them, the whole thing falls to bits.

For whom is the workshop intended?
It is aimed at all client-facing teams. The days of agencies only having client service teams presenting work are not realistic in the multidisciplinary world of digital. Almost always, it's vital to have a strategy person, a client-serviced person, a creative person and a tech person all presenting their relevant part of the pitch. It's important that they all understand the process of storytelling.

One of your first slides in the deck is: 'Listen carefully, then tell them what they want to hear' – can you expand on this?
This is a golden rule. The most important skill when presenting work is to listen to your audience and to focus what you're saying on their feedback, not what you think they want to hear. When things go wrong, it's usually because people have decided how they're going to tell a particular story but don't then gather feedback from the room; for example, if someone is fidgeting or obviously bored yet the presenter ploughs on regardless.

You also may a big point of telling the client something they don't already know. Is that to demonstrate your expertise?
Yes, if you sit down with a smart marketing client and then explain to them how marketing and advertising has changed over the last five years, you end up patronizing them. Finding something that they don't already know is a guaranteed way of surprising them and, yes, showing them that you can lead people on a journey, which is going to be exciting and that they couldn't go on merely by themselves.

WITH A MULTIDISCIPLINARY TEAM, EVERYONE MUST SHARE THE SAME VISION OF STORYTELLING

Industry perspective:
William Lidstone, Razorfish

You talk about the value of creating video research, such as 'vox pops' and eye-tracking studies – why is this important?

When you commit something to video, it has an inherent authenticity. It's the 'as seen on TV' effect. We could present a whole bunch of feedback from a survey or statistics from an eye-tracking study, but the moment we commit them to video it feels more authentic; clients believe in real people and in my experience they pretty much never ever question it.

How do you plan your presentations?

I use white boards and write the story in the first couple of days of receiving the brief so we all know what we've got to do. From here, we'll know what primary research has to be done and will have some idea of the creative content. You know when your presentation is and how long it's going to be so you can work backwards and begin to answer the question. You don't need a huge amount of detail, but enough for everybody to agree that this is the right way forward.

How do you focus your audience's attention and help them remember the detail of a presentation?

I've found that if you manage to get a title or a theme that runs right the way through a story, everything really gels. Sometimes, those come very naturally on day one and that is brilliant. The theme that we followed for DHL was 'Less is More' and we wrote the whole story around it. That was a big story and the presentation was scheduled for three-and-a-half hours. If you can stand up at the beginning of the presentation and say 'We've called this Less is More because of X, Y and Z', it really helps to ground the concept for the client.

Can you explain the rationale for bringing in subject experts to meet the creative team?

I found that it is really useful to bring in subject matter experts to help inform the creative team. We were doing a pitch for a male personal care product, so we invited the Grooming Editor of *GQ Magazine* along and we spent two hours of the pitch talking about trends in male grooming. It was the most useful two hours in the whole pitch. Now what we try and do is bring specific subject matter experts into every pitch environment.

You talk about story archetypal in your deck – what do you mean by this?

There are arguably only seven archetypal stories in the whole world that we listen to. So we get workshop participants to plot and structure a pitch around one of them because clients can easily identify with these stories. There is a basic formula: there is some kind of introduction, there's usually an example of a challenge, a solution is presented and then there is the wrap up.

Can you explain your term 'impress as you go'?

This is really important. I think that people make the biggest mistake by just going away for two weeks and then coming back and saying 'here is the answer...'. You need to generate touchpoints throughout the creative process for clients and make it a very good experience for them.

Your elevator pitch slide is very poignant; is this something you've observed?

Yes. There is, usually in most agencies I've been in, probably about 90 seconds between meeting someone in the reception area and getting them into the boardroom for their presentation. You have 90 seconds which you can so easily prepare for. For instance, you could easily Google the company that are coming in to see you that day and read a news story about something they've recently done, in order to then spend that 90 seconds having a meaningful discussion on a subject that really matters to their business.

A TITLE AND A THEME REALLY HELPS A STORY HAVE FOCUS

195

7.80–7.81 | Storytelling continued
These graphics were created by Razorfish to illustrate William Lidstone's 'storytelling workshop'.

Workshop VII: Perfect pitch

This workshop builds on the presentation strategies outlined in the chapter and on William Lidstone's industry perspective interview to help you deliver an effective presentation. The planning of a presentation may take no more than 30 minutes; however, the actual making of the presentation will take much longer.

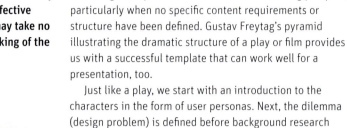

Freytag's pyramid

Climax
(Creative concept)

Rising action
(Research)

Falling action
(Technical approach)

Exposition
(Introduction)

Dénouement
(Summary)

Background

The design of a presentation can be a bewildering prospect, particularly when no specific content requirements or structure have been defined. Gustav Freytag's pyramid illustrating the dramatic structure of a play or film provides us with a successful template that can work well for a presentation, too.

Just like a play, we start with an introduction to the characters in the form of user personas. Next, the dilemma (design problem) is defined before background research and analysis are highlighted. Tension builds towards creating a climax when a solution is presented, followed by a reassuring explanation of how the technical delivery will be achieved before a final summing up – round of applause, the audience is happy, bring down the curtain.

Brief

To design a pitch for a forthcoming presentation or to reconstruct a previous one to see how it could have been done better. For the purposes of this workshop, the presentation should last no more than ten minutes and should incorporate some form of digital presentation tool: for example, Apple Keynote or Microsoft PowerPoint.

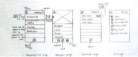

7.83–7.94 | Concept presentation pitch
Usefull by Dustin Roxborough and Santosh Rudra. This is proof of how a concept presentation pitch tackles the issue of food waste in the home through the creation of a mobile app called Usefull. The app helps users keep track of food purchases and use-by dates, and makes helpful recipe suggestions based on this data.

7.82 | Freytag's Pyramid
Gustav Freytag analyzed the dramatic
structure of Greek and Shakespearian
plays, and discovered that most followed
the same five act structure.

Step 1 – Focus on the goal

It is important to be clear from the outset about what
the goal of your presentation is and how you are going to
achieve it. Therefore, ask yourself the following questions
and make note of your answers:

1 What is the purpose of the presentation?
2 Who are we presenting to?
3 What are their expectations?
4 How can the presentation address those needs?
5 Where will we be presenting?
6 What tools will we use?

Step 2 – Reverse engineer

It is often really helpful to reverse engineer your
presentation in order to plan the order of your content.
Start with the last slide and imagine your desired reaction
from the audience at the end of your presentation, and then
work backwards picturing the content and slides that will
need to precede each one.

Step 3 – Arrange the content

Reverse engineering will have given you the building blocks
of your presentation: now you can use Freytag's pyramid to
structure your content in a compelling way.

1 Create a relevant persona or personas for your
   presentation.
2 Outline the design problem and explain key research
   and consumer insights that would inform a solution.
   You may wish to illustrate this with scenarios for your
   persona/s.
3 Your creative concept should be the climax of the
   presentation –excite your audience!
4 Explain your technical approach and include key project
   milestones in the form of a timeline. This reassures the
   client of your capabilities.
5 For the final summary of the pitch, outline any next
   steps and provide any leave-behinds, such as copies of
   the presentation.

Step 4 – Timing

You have been given just ten minutes, so refine your
presentation content by working out how many slides you
can reasonably show and what their key points should be.
You need to capture the audience's attention, then retain it;
a rule of thumb is 30–60 seconds per slide.

If you intend to use video or require a more participatory
demonstration (for example, playing with a new app), the
duration needs to be factored into your presentation.

Step 5 – Provide the script

Successful presentations are seldom unscripted. It is
often helpful to imagine your presentation as a film script
or musical score with your verbal delivery, presentation
images and bullet points as different musical instruments.
As with a musical ensemble, your visual and verbal delivery
should complement, rather than copy, each other.

Scripts are even more critical for team presentations
in order to avoid awkward handovers and to more
effectively distribute presentation responsibilities
between team members.

Good use of presenter notes in Apple Keynote or
Microsoft PowerPoint should be made to reduce the need
for less professional hand-held notes.

Step 6 – Rehearsal

Rehearse to ensure that your points are communicated
effectively and in order to be confident that the purpose of
the presentation has been satisfied. Try to visualize any
curveballs thrown up by an unfamiliar presentation room or
equipment. If you are required to use a different computer
to present with, test your files on someone else's computer
first because it is all too easy to forget to include linked
assets, such as fonts or movies.

The word 'conclusion' tends to suggest that over the course of this book there has been a steady building of a methodical argument towards an inevitable judgement, or that the pieces of a complex puzzle have meticulously been rearranged until it has reached a satisfying completion. However, in the spirit of participation, or interaction if you will, I want to ask you – what do you feel is the natural conclusion?

To try and summarize the learning in this book, it began with the very basics of how to research interactive projects and explained some useful design development processes. It touched on the complexities of semiotics and integrated the timeless principles of typography and layout with the latest digital practice. It has showcased a wide variety of interactive and design projects, and discussed some of the key concepts and principles of interaction that underpin them. It has also attempted to give insight into how to effectively present design and interactive work.

Over the course of nearly 200 pages and 600 images, this book has featured the work of many individuals, groups, large agencies and small studios from around the world, some of whom are famous, others relatively unknown. Not all of the work featured is interactive, nor is all of it award-winning, but what binds it together is that it is all good work that exemplifies great practice and a dedication to getting things right.

With all this content covered, I hope that the subject of interactive design has been made clearer, and that it appears a little magical and not so shrouded in mystery. I hope that research is seen as a creative process and that we work with personable users, not faceless audiences. I hope that new developments in technology are not so daunting, but inspire new creative opportunities, and the tools we use to design great projects involve interaction with people as much as the need to hone digital craft skills.

Above all, I hope that the experience of reading these chapters has conjured not just thoughts but feelings and that, just as with interactive design itself, this book has been both useful and pleasurable.

Conclusion

8.01–8.08 | Audi City
Audi City cyberstore by Razorfish. The brand's entire model line-up presented fully and digitally in a compact space. With the newly created position of Customer Relationship Manager, visitors can expect an even more personal level of consultation and assistance with individual services. As an urban meeting point, Audi City will also reinforce dialogue between people and the brand.

Glossary

3D printing is an additive manufacturing process where a three-dimensional object is created from a digital model. The object is gradually built-up from the successive layering of new material.

Affordance is a design principle, where the apparent and actual properties of an object give a visual clue as to how it can be used.

Agile development is a fast and flexible software development method that gives cross-disciplinary teams the autonomy to make timely decisions in response to change as part of an ongoing iterative design process.

Animatics are storyboard images or more polished visuals sequenced in a video-editing package with sample music to give a better sense of timing and creative intention.

Back channelling is the use of technology to provide a real-time web forum, live chat, tweeting or other messaging service alongside a primary activity, such, as a live TV show.

The **cloud** is a term used to refer to a personal or shared online file space used for storing data.

A **comp** is short for 'comprehensive layout', which is presented to clients to give an idea of the proposed design prior to final images and copy (written text) being supplied.

A **comping image** is a low-resolution placeholder used in layout.

A **concept** is an abstracted or refined idea that addresses the needs of a particular issue or problem. See 'idea' for a linked definition.

Copy is a term used to describe written material used in a design layout.

CSS3 (Cascading Style Sheets version 3) is a language designed for the presentation or formatting of HTML or XML content. This latest version contains more advanced features that enhance the look and feel of content; for example, increase the page elements on rollover and round corner boxes.

D1 is a digital video standard (PAL 720x576, NTSC 720x486). When introduced in 1986, D1 referred to the large digital video cassette on which uncompressed digital video was stored.

DV is a later digital video format introduced in 1995 and is the same resolution as D1 in PAL, and slightly different for NTSC – 720x480.

Ethnography is the study of people and their cultures. Ethnographic research is qualitative method that relies on observation and interaction with the person or people being studied over a long period of time.

Feature phones are low-end mobile phones that have capabilities beyond a basic mobile phone, such as limited web browsing, MP3 playback and camera.

Flow is a mental state where the task set is equally matched by the person's skills, fully immersing them in the moment, making them feel energized and absorbed. Mihály Csíkszentmihályi first proposed this psychological concept.

Frame rate is the frequency of sequential image frames displayed every second. Cinema films display images at 24 frames per second (fps), NTSC television at 29.97fps, PAL and SECAM at 25fps.

Gamification is the integration of game dynamics or mechanics in non-game related businesses or content in order to increase participation and engagement.

HDTV is High Definition Television. There are currently two resolutions: 1280x720 and 1920x1080. However, the lower resolution is being phased out with the introduction of the latest television sets.

HTML5 is the latest iteration of Hypertext Mark-up Language (HTML), which has better support for multimedia content including audio, video, web apps and advanced graphics. It also supports geolocation, which allows you to share your location with trusted websites to give you advanced services.

An **idea** is an undiluted or unmoderated plan, proposal or suggestion often generated during a brainstorming session. See 'concept' for a linked definition.

Ident is a short animation or video revealing a channel's identity.

An **information architect** labels, organizes and structures information to create interactive products and experiences that are intuitive and usable.

An **interaction designer** designs the behaviour of interactive systems. Interaction designers strive to create meaningful relationships between people and the products and services that they use.

IPTV (Internet Protocol Television) is a system through which services such as live TV, catch-up and video on demand (VOD) are delivered over the Internet. Although it uses the Internet to stream media content, it differs from Internet television in that it is delivered through a set-top box attached to a television, and is usually a subscription service.

Iterative design is a design methodology whereby every phase of design prototyping is tested, analysed and refined as part of a continual cycle of development.

Lossless encoding uses a data compression algorithm that retains all original data when compressed so that no data is discarded.

Lossy is an encoding method that compresses files by discarding data.

Modding is a slang term for 'modifying', and usually refers to the modifying of hardware and software – for example, the building of user-generated game levels.

Parallax scrolling is a visual technique used to give the illusion of images living in a three-dimensional space. In web design, the illusion is perceived when the user scrolls, causing layered foreground images to move faster than the background image.

Photo libraries supply stock images to designers and license them for specific uses. They are used as a creative alternative to commissioning photographers or illustrators. Photo libraries can be accessed and searched online. Popular photo libraries online include: *123rf.com*, *corbisimages.com*, *gettyimages. com*, *istockphoto.com* and *shutterstock.com*.

Pro formas are forms used to capture essential information about a design project, or statements used to provide clients with an itemized bill of design services.

Qualitative research is a method of inquiry concerned with understanding why social phenomena occur, rather than gather quantitative statistical data about what has happened. Qualitative researchers usually study things in their own environment, and attempt to interpret meaning given to social phenomena by people and understand behavioural patterns that occur because of them.

Quantitative research refers to the methodical gathering of data about social phenomena in numerical form. The data can be put into categories, or in rank order, or displayed in units of measurement and then used to construct graphs and tables for further analysis.

SDTV is Standard Definition Television. This is the common broadcast resolution received by television without high-definition capability or reception (PAL 720x576 and NTSC 720x486).

Smartphones are high-end mobile phones that have advanced computing ability, allowing the user to browse the Internet, download games and use more complex applications (for example, word processors and spreadsheets).

Sting is a short promotional advert for an individual programme, channel or season of programming usually lasting between 10–30 seconds.

Seven mass media the phrase 'seventh mass media channel' was coined in 2006 by Tomi Ahonen, a telecommunications consultant and author, to draw attention to the unique benefits of the latest generation of mobile phones. The seven mass media in chronological order are:
1. Print – late fifteenth century, 2. Recordings (Audio) – late nineteenth century, 3. Cinema – c.1900, 4. Radio – c.1910, 5. Television – c.1950, 6. Internet – c.1990, 7. Mobile – c.2000.

Bibliography

Title sequence is an animated or video based introduction to a television programme or film revealing the title and main credits.

A **site map** has two definitions in interactive design: First, it is a list of pages on a website used to help users navigate and search a site's content. Second, it is a diagram providing an overview of a website or applications structure used to help plan an interactive design.

A **skeuomorph** is the embellishment of a new design with the decorative form or aesthetic of an old design. Skeuomorphs are deliberately employed to make a new design appear familiar and attractive to the user.

User experience (UX) refers to how someone uses a product, service or system. The two most important requisites of user experience are whether it meets their functional requirements and how satisfying was their experience of using it.

A **user interface designer** designs the visual 'front end' or interface of a product or service. A 'UI' designer usually has a background in graphic design.

A **user experience designer** collectively oversees the information architecture, interaction design and user interface design of a system or application.

The **user experience design pattern** or UX Pattern, is an established pattern of use or solution to common problems for the user, for example, the organization or structure of an app or the established gestures used for a touch-screen mobile phone.

The **user interface design pattern** or UI Pattern, is an established solution to a common interface problem, for example, the use of breadcrumb trails to aid naivgation or the on-screen entry of a house number and postcode or zipcode to help fill out the address details of a user.

Viewport is a rectangular window or viewing region used to display graphics. In web design, the viewport size commonly refers to the width of the browser window available to show pages. At various viewport sizes, a web design can 'snap' to fit using different layouts in order to better display web page content.

Web 2.0 refers to a change in vision for The Web rather than a new technical standard. The term was coined by Tim O'Reilly in 2004 and refers to websites and technologies that encourage users to interact and communicate with each other through social media and user-generated content.

Web fonts are display fonts often accessed through online type foundries and displayed though web browsers. Web fonts allow designers much more choice and control over the fonts that are used because they no longer rely on the user owning the license. Many type foundries now license web versions of their fonts for this use.

YouView is a hybrid set-top box with both a broadband connection and television antenna allowing access to TV catch-up and Freeview content in the UK.

Allan, D., Kingdon, M., Murrin, K. and Rudkin, D. (2002) *Sticky wisdom*. 2nd edn. Oxford: Capstone.

Ambrose, G. and Harris, P. (2005) *Colour*. Lausanne: AVA.

Arden, P. (2003) *It's not how good you are, it's how good you want to be*. London: Phaidon.

Armstrong, H. (2009) *Graphic design theory: readings from the field*. New York: Princeton Architectural.

Austin, T. and Doust, R. (2007) *New media design*. London: Laurence King.

Barthes, R. (1967) *Elements of semiology*. London: Cape.

Bayley, S. and Mavity, R. (2007) *Life's a pitch: how to be business-like with your emotional life and emotional with your business life*. London: Bantam.

Bringhurst, R. (2004) *The elements of typographic style*. 3rd edn. Point Roberts, WA: Hartley & Marks.

Brody, D. and Clark, H. (2009) *Design studies: a reader*. New York: Berg.

Burrough, X. and Mandiberg, M. (2009) *Digital foundations: intro to media design with the Adobe creative suite*. Berkeley, CA: New Riders.

Carter, R. (2002) *Digital color and type*. Hove: RotoVision.

Cohn, M. (2004) *User stories applied: for agile software development*. London: Addison-Wesley.

Collins, H. (2010) *Creative research: the theory and practice of research for the creative industries*. Lausanne: AVA Academia.

Cooper, A. Reimann, R. and Cronin, D. (2009) *About Face 3.0: the essentials of interaction design*. 3rd edn. Indianapolis, IN: Wiley.

Creeber, G. and Martin, R. (2009) *Digital cultures*. Maidenhead: Open University Press.

Cross, N. (2011) *Design thinking: understanding how designers think and work*. Oxford: Berg.

Crow, D. (2010) *Visible signs: an introduction to semiotics in the visuals arts*. Lausanne: AVA.

De Bono, E. (2009) *Six thinking hats*. London: Penguin.

Fling, B. (2009) *Mobile design and development*. 1st edn. Beijing; Sebastopol, CA: O'Reilly.

Fraser, T. and Banks, A. (2010) *Colour in design*. Lewes: Ilex.

Hall, S. (2012) *This means this, this means that: a user's guide to semiotics*. 2nd edn. London: Laurence King.

Heller, S. and Womack, D. (2008) *Becoming a digital designer: a guide to careers in web, video, broadcast, game and animation design*. Chichester: John Wiley.

Hill, W. (2010) *The complete typographer: a foundation course for graphic designers working with type*. 3rd edn. London: Thames & Hudson.

Kane, J. (2011) *A type primer*. 2nd edn. London: Laurence King.

Lewandowsky, P. and. Zeischegg, F. (2003) *A practical guide to digital design*. Lausanne: AVA.

Lister, M. (2009) *New media: a critical introduction*. 2nd edn. London: Routledge.

Lupton, E. (2010) *Thinking with type: a critical guide for designers, writers, editors, and students*. 2nd edn. New York: Princeton Architectural Press.

Lupton, E. (2011) *Graphic design thinking: beyond brainstorming*. Enfield: Publishers Group UK.

McCandless, D. (2010) *Information is beautiful*. London: HarperCollins.

McCormack, L. (2005) *Designers are wankers*. London: About Face.

Maeda, J. (2006) *The laws of simplicity*. Cambridge, MA: MIT Press.

Martin, B. and Hanington, B. (2012) *Universal methods of design: 100 ways to research complex problems, develop innovative ideas, and design effective solutions*. Beverly, MA: Rockport Publishers.

Moggridge, B. (2010) *Designing media*. London: MIT Press.

Morville, P. and Rosenfeld, L. (2007) *Information architecture for the World Wide Web*. 3rd edn. Beijing; Farnham: O'Reilly.

Müller-Brockman, J. (2008) *The grid system in graphic design: a handbook for graphic artists, typographers, and exhibition designers*. 6th edn. Sulgen: Niggli.

Norman, D. (2004) *Emotional design: why we love (or hate) everyday things*. New York: Basic Books.

Pressdy, S. (2004) *How to market design consultancy services: finding, winning, keeping and developing clients*. 2nd edn. Aldershot: Gower.

Samara T. (2005) *Making and breaking the grid: a graphic design layout workshop*. Gloucester, MA: Rockport.

Stickdorn, M. and Schneider, J. (2010) *This is service design thinking: basics, tools, cases*. Amsterdam: BIS.

Taylor, A. (2011) *Design essentials for the motion media artist: a practical guide to principles and techniques*. Burlington, MA: Focal Press.

Unger, R. and Chandler, C. (2008) *A project guide to UX design: for user experience designers in the field or in the making*. 2nd edn. Berkeley, CA: New Riders.

Van Dijck, P. (2003) *Information architecture for designers: structuring websites for business success*. Hove: RotoVision.

Visocky O'Grady, J. and Visocky O'Grady, K. (2006) *A designer's research manual: succeed in design*. Hove: RotoVision.

Web references

Arthur, C. (2011) *How the Smartphone is Killing the PC. The Guardian*. Available at: *http://www.guardian.co.uk/technology/2011/jun/05/smartphones-killing-pc* (Accessed: 25 November 2012).

Brandon, J. (2010) *Understanding the Z-Layout in Web Design*. Available at: *http://webdesign.tutsplus.com/articles/design-theory/understanding-the-z-layout-in-web-design/* (Accessed: 24 November 2012).

Browser Display Statistics. Available at: *http://www.w3schools.com/browsers/browsers_display.asp* (Accessed: 1 October 2012).

Canalys (2012) *Smartphones Overtake Client PCs in 2011*. Available at: *http://www.canalys.com/newsroom/smart-phones-overtake-client-pcs-2011* (Accessed: 25 November 2012).

Cisco Visual Networking Index: Forecast and Methodology, 2011-2016. Cisco. Available at: *http://www.cisco.com/en/US/solutions/collateral/ns341/ns525/ns537/ns705/ns827/white_paper_c11-481360_ns827_Networking_Solutions_White_Paper.html* (Accessed: 10 Jan 2013).

Contrast (Minimum): Understanding SC 1.4.3. Available at: *http://www.w3.org/TR/UNDERSTANDING-WCAG20/visual-audio-contrast-contrast.html* (Accessed: 15 Mar 2013).

Exon, M. and Flood, R. (2010) *Design Industry Insights*. Design Council. Available at: *http://www.designcouncil.org.uk/publications/industry-insights-2010/* (Accessed: 10 Jan 2013).

Gestalt psychology (2012). Available at: *http://en.wikipedia.org/wiki/Gestalt_psychology* (Accessed: 23 November 2012).

Govan, P. (2008-01-23) *Older Family Gaming Market*. Available at: *http://www.gamepeople.co.uk/familygamer0105.htm* (Accessed: 15 Mar 2013).

How to Calculate Color Contrast from RGB Values. Available at: *http://www.had2know.com/technology/color-contrast-calculator-web-design.html* (Accessed: 15 Mar 2013).

IBOPE (2012) *In Brazil, 43% of Internet Users Watch TV While Surfing*. Available at: *http://www.ibope.com.br/pt-br/relacionamento/imprensa/releases/Paginas/No-Brasil-43-dos-internautas-assistem-a-TV-enquanto-navegam.aspx* (Accessed: 15 Mar 2013).

Johnston, J. (2010) *The Grid System Made Easy*. Available at: *http://sixrevisions.com/web_design/the-960-grid-system-made-easy/* (Accessed: 15 Mar 2013).

Jones, M. (2011) *Designing Games Interfaces*. Available at: *http://www.slideshare.net/FlashGen/designing-game-interfaces* (Accessed: 15 Mar 2013).

Lupton, E. (2004) *Deconstruction and Graphic Design: History Meets Theory*. Available at: *http://www.typotheque.com/articles/deconstruction_and_graphic_design_history_meets_theory* (Accessed: 23 November 2012).

Nielsen, J. (2001) *First Rule of Usability? Don't Listen to Users*. Available at: *http://www.nngroup.com/articles/first-rule-of-usability-dont-listen-to-users/* (Accessed: 15 Mar 2013).

Nielsen, J. (2006) *F-Shaped Pattern for Reading Web Content. Jakob Nielsen's Alertbox*. Available at: *http://www.useit.com/alertbox/reading_pattern.html* (Accessed: 12 November 2012).

Shaikh, A.D. (2005) *The Effects of Line Length on Reading Online News*. Available at: *http://www.surl.org/usabilitynews/72/LineLength.asp* (Accessed: 20 Feb 2013).

Shearman, S. (2011) *Heineken Rolls Out StarPlayer Football Game*. Available at: *http://www.marketingmagazine.co.uk/news/1067169/* (Accessed: 15 Mar 2013).

Sherman, C. (2005) *A New F-Word for Google Search Results. Search Engine Watch*. Available at: http://searchenginewatch.com/article/2066806/A-New-F-Word-for-Google-Search-Results (Accessed: 12 November 2012).

The Crystal Goblet. (2012) Available at: http://en.wikipedia.org/wiki/The_Crystal_Goblet (Accessed: 23 November 2012).

User Experience Guides (2012) *iOS Development Library*. Available at: *http://developer.apple.com/library/ios/#documentation/userexperience/conceptual/mobilehig/UEBestPractices/UEBestPractices.html* (Accessed: 25 November 2012).

Yahoo and Nielsen Convergence Panel (2010) *The American Media Multi-Tasker Study*. Available at: *http://advertising.yahoo.com/article/insight-the-american-media-multitasker.html* (Accessed: 25 November 2012).

Wolverton, T. (2007) *Women Driving 'Casual Game' Boom*. Available at: *http://www.mercurynews.com/ci_6695921* (Accessed: 15 Mar 2013).

Useful resources

Interactive design is an interdisciplinary subject drawing on a wide variety of knowledge and expertise, so the design and development resources are plentiful. The bibliography section provides a list of useful books and articles for further reading on interactive design allowing this section to focus on useful tools and online resources:

App prototyping tools
appinseconds.com
balsamiq.com
justinmind.com
invisionapp.com
popapp.in
proto.io

Bookmarking tools
delicious.com
digg.com
pintrest.com
reddit.com
stumbleupon.com
twitter.com

Card sorting and tools
optimalworkshop.com/optimalsort.htm
simplecardsort.com/
sixrevisions.com/usabilityaccessibility/card-sorting/
userzoom.com/products/card-sorting
uxpunk.com/websort/
xsortapp.com/

Colour
colorschemedesigner.com
colorsontheweb.com
colourlovers.com
kuler.adobe.com
pictaculous.com
web.colorotate.org

Communal websites
behance.net
carbonmade.com
designrelated.com
deviantart.com
dribbble.com
hunie.co

Design inspiration
artofthetitle.com
awwwards.com
designarchives.aiga.org
dribbble.com
stumbleupon.com
thefwa.com

Design portfolios
behance.net
carbonmade.com
cargocollective.com
deviantart.com
sohosoho.tv
topinteractiveagencies.com

Grids and layout
960.gs
bbc.co.uk/gel
cssgrid.net
designinfluences.com/fluid960gs
semantic.gs
thegridsystem.org

Illustrators and photographers
agencyrush.com
contactacreative.com
eyemade.com
handsomefrank.com
horton-stephens.com
magnumphotos.com

Image libraries
123rf.com
corbisimages.com
fotolia.com
gettyimages.com
istockphoto.com
shutterstock.com

Motion graphics
artofthetitle.com
awn.com
motionographer.com
motionserved.com
motionspire.com
videocopilot.net

Popular analytics tools
alexa.com/toolbar
clicky.com
crazyegg.com
google.com/analytics
haveamint.com
woopra.com

Template-based content management systems
blogger.com
cargocollective.com
drupal.org
indexhibit.org
joomla.co.uk
vbulletin.com

Typography
ilovetypography.com
tdc.org
typographica.org
typophile.com
webtypography.net
welovetypography.com

Type foundries and web fonts
fonts.com
fontfont.com
google.com/webfonts
playtype.com
processtypefoundry.com
typekit.com

UI design patterns
graffletopia.com
konigi.com
patternry.com
patterntap.com
ui-patterns.com
welie.com

User experience
boxesandarrows.com
iainstitute.org
nngroup.com
usability.gov
uxbooth.com
uxmatters.com

Web authoring tools
Adobe Dreamweaver: *adobe.com/dreamweaver*
Coda2: *panic.com/coda*
Expression Web: *microsoft.com/expression/*
HTML Editor: *coffeecup.com/html-editor*
Komodo Edit: *activestate.com/komodo-edit*
TextEdit: *apple.com*

Web design
24ways.org
alistapart.com
netmagazine.com
smashingmagazine.com
thenextweb.com
w3schools.com

Wireframing tools
Adobe InDesign: *adobe.com/indesign*
Adobe Illustrator: *adobe.com/illustrator*
axure.com
balsamiq.com
Microsoft PowerPoint: *office.microsoft.com*
protoshare.com

Guidelines
Android design guidelines for app development: *developer.android.com/design/index.html*
Apple's human interface guidelines for iOS app development: *developer.apple.com/library/ios/#documentation/UserExperience/Conceptual/MobileHIG/Introduction/Introduction.html*
BBC's Global Experience Language design guidelines for television and web: *bbc.co.uk/gel/*
Internet Advertising Bureau provides guidelines and supports creative standards: *iab.net*
Microsoft's usability guidelines: *msdn.microsoft.com/en-us/library/bb158578.aspx*

The World Wide Web Consortium governs web standards and provides guidelines and resources for web design and development: *w3.org*

Index

204

Picture credits

Images courtesy of: © 2013 with express permission from Adobe Systems Incorporated: 74 | AKQA: 161, 166, 167 | Amazon: 109 | artqu/123RF Stock Photo: 82 | Audi AG: 199 | AllofUs/Yota Play: 145 | Timo Arnall, BERG (bergcloud.com): 9 | bagiuiani/123RF Stock Photo: 82 | Bibliothèque Design: 6, 84, 85, 86, 87 | Blacknegative: 149 | Boondoggle : 150 | Bridgeman: 119 | Mark Blythe: 36 | British Broadcasting Corporation (BBC): 56, 73, 100, 102, 170, 171, 172, 173 | © 2013 CIID 213: 26, 27, 28, 29, 40, 41 | Jason Bishop, © Sony Electronics Corp.: 108 | Cienpies/123RF Stock Photo: 82 | Rob Cleaton : 22, 23 | Courtesy of Carte Blanche Films: 101 | Ryan Coupe, Luke Emmerson, David Ingledow: 176, 182, 183 | © Channel Four Television Corporation: 164, 165 | Matt Chea, 2009: 121 | cokemomo/123RF Stock Photo: 88 | © ColorSchemeDesigner.com: 74 | Image Copyright Arno van Dulmen, 2013 Used under license from Shutterstock.com: 77 | Dare: 33 | Dribbble LLC: 24 | Edenspiekermann: 46, 47, 58, 98, 134, 135, 186, 187 | Dead Space 3 images used with permission of Electronic Arts, Inc.: 156 | Mirror's Edge images used with permission of Electronic Arts, Inc.: 157 | Luke Emmerson: 84, 85 | Husam Elfaki: 176, 188 | elisanth/123RF Stock Photo: 82 | e-Types/Playtype: 11, 91, 106, 107, 110, 111, 112, 113 | Fairly Painless Advertising and Imaginary Forces: 80 | FontShop AG: 94, 95, 96 | Lise Gagne/123RF Stock Photo: 78 | Garbergs: 151 | Gardiner-Richardson: 184, 185 | Getty Images: 83, 118 | Zara Gonzalez Hoang: 34 | Google and the Google logo are registered trademarks of Google Inc., used with permission: 18 | Maylin Gouldie/Red Bee, maylingouldie.co.uk: 56 | Max Holford: 175 | Max Holford, David Ingledow, Ella Rasmussen: 30, 31 | hypermania2/123RF Stock Photo: 88 | © Hattula Moholy Nagy/DACS 2013: 119 | © Image & Form: 158 | ©iStockphoto.com/ilbusca: 77 | ©iStockphoto.com/RypeArts: 77 | David Ingledow: 143 | © Kinetic Design & Advertising Pte Limited: 11, 117 | Komodo Digital: 50, 51, 81, 129, 132, 133, 146, 147, 152, 153, 180, 181 | Kotoc: 159 | Igor Mitin: 76 | McKinney and Urban Ministries of Durham: 104 | Mahifx.com: 105 | David McCandless and Always With Honor, InformationisBeautiful.net: 68 | © Katherine McCoy/ Photography by Robert Hensleigh and Tim Thayer: 120 | James Medcraft/onedotzero: 168, 169 | A Milk+Koblin Project, copyright: Chris Milk, and Aaron Koblin, Google: Cover, 148 | Moving Brands: 10, 20, 21, 48, 49, 60, 61, 62, 63, 70, 178, 179 | Müller-Brockmann, Josef (b. 1914): Weniger Lärm (Less Noise), 10 x 12 (1) (A) 1960. New York, Museum of Modern Art (MoMA). Offset lithograph, printed in colour, 50 1/4 x 35 1/2' (127.6 x 90.1 cm). Acquired by exchange. 513.1983 © 2013. Digital image, The Museum of Modern Art, New York/Scala, Florence: 120 | Nation London Ltd.: 69, 117, 127 | Nordkapp: 13, 14, 43, 52, 53, 54, 55 | oksun70/123RF Stock Photo: 88 | Onformative/Interbrand: 10, 67 | Plump Digital: 13, 17, 19, 44, 131, 154 | Julius Popp: 103 | Precedent: 38, 39 | Preloaded: 155 | Proud Creative Limited: 162, 163 | Psyop: 72 | Paul Rand Revocable Trust: 120 | Razorfish: 192, 193, 194, 195 | Reactive: 79, 122, 123, 124 | Santosh Rudra: 115 | Santosh Rudra , Dustin Roxborough: 196, 197 | Lukas Schrank: 177, 190, 191 | Spotify: 8 | Jamie Steane: 16, 18, 25, 35, 64, 65, 131, 136 | SurveyMonkey: 17 | Tschichold, Jan (1902-1974): Die Frau ohne Name (The Woman Without Digitale (1)(A) a Name), 1927. New York, Museum of Modern Art (MoMA). Offset lithograph, 48 3/4 x 34' (123.8 x 86.4 cm). Peter Stone Poster Fund. Acc. n.: 225.1978.© 2013. Digital image, The Museum of Modern Art, New York/Scala, Florence: 119 | TrueView: 138, 139, 140, 141 | Will Tunstall, Chris Edwards and Marcus Foley: 75 | Uber Digital: 57 | Designed by April Greiman & Jayme Odgers; Photography by Guy Webster; Art Direction by Leonard Koren. Copyright © 1979 Wet Magazine (Leonard Koren): 120 | Weingart, Wolfgang (b. 1941): Typographic Process, Nr 4. Digitale 93 (1)(A) Typographic Signs, 1971-72.. New York, Museum of Modern Art (MoMA). Lithograph, 34 1/2 x 24 1/4' (87.6 x 61.6 cm). Printer: G. Gissler Basle. Juerg Zumtobel Purchase Fund. Acc. n.: 264.2002.4.© 2013. Digital image, The Museum of Modern Art, New York/ Scala, Florence: 120 | YossarianLives!: 45 | © Zeebox: 160

All reasonable attempts have been made to trace, clear and credit the copyright holders of the images reproduced in this book. However, if any credits have been inadvertently omitted, the publisher will endeavour to incorporate amendments in future editions.

Acknowledgements and credits

This book is based on 20 years' worth of professional procrastination and a year of intense research and writing activity. It would not have been possible without the encouragement and gentle prodding of Trevor Duncan, Janine Munslow and Joyce Yee at Northumbria University or the professional perspective of Dan Edwards. This book would certainly have been impossible without the love and support of J.O.V.E. – Jamie, Ollie, Vashti and Esme xxx.

At Bloomsbury, I owe thanks to Georgia Kennedy for commissioning the book in the first place, a huge debt to Colette Meacher and Lucy Tipton for their patience and tireless help in getting this book written, and finally to Roger Fawcett-Tang who has had to work with my innumerable design suggestions.

There are a number of contributors to whom I owe particular thanks:

Dan Baker, Precedent, Perth
Charles Batho, London
Tim Beard, Bibliothèque, London
Jason Bishop, Los Angeles
James Bull, Moving Brands, Los Angeles
Paul Canty, Preloaded, London
James Chorley, AKQA, London
Rob Cleaton, London
Rob Colley, Plump Digital, York
Steven Cook, Edenspiekermann, Berlin
Lizzie Dewhurst, AKQA, London
Eilidh Dickson, CIID Consulting, Copenhagen
Vanessa Diéguez, Kotoc Productions, Barcelona
Rebecca Duddridge, Uber Digital, London
Husam Elfaki, AKQA, London
Karin Fong, Imaginary Forces, New York
Daniel Foster-Smith, Yossarian Lives!, London
Andy Greener, Komodo Digital, Newcastle-upon-Tyne
Tom Kile Hartshorn, Nation, London
Emma Jefferies, Newcastle-upon-Tyne
Mathias Jespersen, e-Types, Copenhagen
Panu Korhonen, Nordkapp, Helsinki
John Lau, Preloaded, London
Julia Laub, Onformative, Berlin
William Lidstone, Razorfish, London
Christian Meldgaard, e-Types, Copenhagen
Georgina Milne, Moving Brands, London
Sami Niemelä, Nordkapp, Helsinki
Campbell Orme, Moving Brands, London
Adam Quickfall, Peg Digital, Newcastle-upon-Tyne
Darren Richardson, Gardiner-Richardson, Newcastle-upon-Tyne
Paul Robinson, Uber Digital, London
Helle Rohde Andersen, CIID Consulting, Copenhagen
Lukas Schrank, Sydney
Katrina Scott, Reactive, New York
Mark Sherwin, Precedent, London
Jürgen Siebert, Fontshop, Berlin
Matt Verity, TrueView, London
Dunja Vitolic, Imaginary Forces, Los Angeles
Shane Walter, onedotzero, London

Finally, additional thanks to some of my graduating and continuing students at Northumbria University for their individual contributions: Ana Breso-Gonzalez, Oscar Chui, Ryan Coupe, Luke Emmerson, Max Holford, David Ingledow, Dustin Roxborough and Santosh Rudra.

208